Play like a

Pirate

Engage Students with
Toys, Games, and Comics

Make Your Classroom

Fun Again!

By

Quinn Rollins

PLAY LIKE A PIRATE

©2016 by Quinn Rollins

This book is available at special discounts when purchased in quantity for use as premiums, promotions, fundraising, and educational use. For inquiries and details, contact us: shelley@daveburgessconsulting.com.

Published by Dave Burgess Consulting, Inc.
San Diego, CA
http://daveburgessconsulting.com

Cover Design by Genesis Kohler
Editing and Interior Design by My Writers' Connection
About the Author and About the Duck photos by Randy Archibald

Library of Congress Control Number: 2016931719
Paperback ISBN: 978-0-9861555-4-3
E-book ISBN: 978-0-9861555-5-0

First Printing: February 2016

CONTENTS

INTRODUCTION

I've always wanted to be a teacher. Some of my earliest memories are of setting up a tiny classroom with my teddy bear, stuffed duck, and a stuffed mouse. They'd all sit at little box desks, and I'd hand out assignments to them. I'd do their work for them (they couldn't do it; they were toys), correct it, and give it back. Sadly, Mouse never mastered some important concepts, but Bear and Duckie did pretty well, considering their limitations. Some of my key ideas, and especially my feelings, about teaching were shaped before I actually went to school. My older sister's tales about her class and *Sesame Street* gave me an idea of what school should be like.

When *Sesame Street* first started production in the late 1960s, it was, in many ways, revolutionary. Combining puppets, animation, live action, music, and comedy into one program had been experimented with before. But doing so with the explicit goal of educating children—and specifically low-income and minority children? That was new. Joan Ganz Cooney organized people from education, music, puppetry, and animation to make something that wasn't pedantic. It was fun! An animated, psychedelic pinball game that counts to twelve? Enthralling! Grover demonstrating "near" and "far" until he collapses into a pile of blue fur? Hilarious! Ernie singing about his "Rubber Duckie"? Okay,

I honestly don't get the educational value of that one, but it kept me tuning in every day.

Isn't that what we want for our students—for them to be tuned in? For them to *want* to come to our classes, even if they weren't forced to come? As a classroom teacher, I've found that the more fun I'm having, the more fun my students are having. With the panicked push to "teach to the test," a lot of teachers forget their own earliest lessons: teaching and learning should be fun. And engaged kids (the ones having the fun) are more likely to actually learn. If I'm bored by an assignment, students are bored, too. The worst kinds of days are when I notice midday how bored I am—and how bored they are—but keep plowing on through anyway. How miserable for me! How miserable for them! But some teachers in every school in every subject turn teaching into a chore nine months out of the year. A chore, like something you'd do on a farm! To them, school registers on the same fun level as harvesting crops, milking cows, petting chickens, or anything else that city boys, like me, know so little about.

"Chore" is how I'd describe most of my classes as a kid, particularly my history classes. As a rule, we either sat through ninety minutes of lecture or read a chapter and answered the questions at the end of it. Occasionally, we watched a video and wrote one hundred facts (in complete sentences, of course) or colored a map, which for me meant doodling spaceships and robots in the margins after I finished the coloring. But there were exceptions, teachers who actually taught. Because of them, I *did* learn, and my experience as a student didn't kill my love of learning or school.

When I became a teacher, I knew I wanted to give my students better learning experiences than I'd had. I wanted to move past the worksheets and *chapterized* formula that killed so many history classes for me. I wanted to make education entertaining. But how?

I found the answer to that question in my toy box at home. Toys. What could be more fun?

Three years ago, I discovered Dave Burgess' book, *Teach Like a PIRATE*. (If you haven't read it yet, you need to. Buy a copy of his book and then one for a friend. And then buy ten more copies of my book because you have friends who need birthday presents.) Dave is amazing—inspiring in person and in print. The big takeaway from his book is that teachers need to use their passion in the classroom. That

wasn't a new message for me—I'd been doing it for years. But his book legitimized what I was trying to do. I hope you have passion about the content you teach. My passions are history, science, and reading. I love them all. And they combine to fit into my classes pretty nicely. I also have passion for great pedagogy. I've worked with and learned from teachers who are geniuses—teachers who make my efforts seem fit only for teaching teddy bears and stuffed ducks. But I learn from them and use their best ideas to teach my own students.

In his book, Burgess writes about the passions too many of us leave at home—passions we mistakenly believe have nothing to do with our jobs. Music, cooking, sports, movies, video games, gardening, architecture—all the things we adults do to blow off steam, the obsessions we have, the things that make us happy when we're doing them, the things that make us feel like *us*—those are the things we should be bringing into the classroom. *Teach Like a PIRATE* reminded me that bringing those passions to work invites happiness into the classroom, as well. Your enthusiasm will energize your teaching, and whether or not your kids share the same passion as you, your excitement will be contagious.

My passion? Toys. Most of us loved toys at some point in our lives. My love of toys started with the Fisher-Price® Little People Play Family, those little peg-shaped people who had a mooing barn and a schoolhouse with a ringing bell on top. You could even turn the Little People into finger puppets and have an entirely different way to play with them. Ah, Little People. They were the best. By 1978 (I really am old, you guys), I dumped Little People for *Star Wars* action figures, which I loved to a point bordering on idol worship (okay, superseding idol worship). This continued through about 1985 when I reached the age where I could either grow out of playing with toys or latch onto something new. That's when I met LEGO®. I'll gush about LEGO later

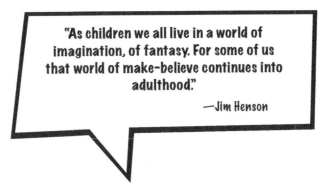

"As children we all live in a world of imagination, of fantasy. For some of us that world of make-believe continues into adulthood."

—Jim Henson

in this book. (In fact, my unabashed love for LEGO may make some of you dear readers uncomfortable.) For now, I'll leave it at this: I *love* LEGO. More than any adult should. There have been other series of action figures I've loved. In my college years, *Star Trek* action figures were a favorite, as were Muppets and an animated-style Justice League line. According to some people (especially the person I'm married to), I could quite possibly have a "toy problem." I collect toys, I play with toys, and I make my own toys. Lest you (or my wife) think toys are only all fun and games, I've discovered countless ways that taking my love of toys into the classroom has helped me become a better teacher *and* actually enjoy teaching.

Some people think being seen as the "fun teacher" carries some risk. The worry is that, if you're fun, you'll never have the respect of your students, their parents, or your administrators. In my opinion, if that's your concern, you probably have bigger problems than LEGO can solve. The biggest risk with making your class fun is your students are more likely to be engaged and get on your side. With them on your side, you'll be taking them somewhere. You can be the fun teacher *and* teach them great content. You can have rigorous instruction taking place in a fun classroom. Another risk you face as the fun teacher is that your students will go to their other classes and tell their friends they had fun in your class. Terrible! And at the end of the day when their parents ask what they did in school, they'll actually remember! They'll remember the fun they had *and* what they actually learned, and their younger siblings will look at them with Shakespearean-like jealousy. Yep, being the fun teacher definitely carries some risk!

Your class should be the class students look forward to—the one they would ditch another teacher's class for. Don't let them do that; but it's okay to feel a little pride knowing they want to stay in your class all day. As Dave Burgess puts it, you should be able to sell tickets to your lessons. I can't say I hit that target every day, but when I do, it's because I'm doing something unconventional and incorporating my own personal passions into the lesson.

You are a teacher and a professional, so I'm assuming you know how to use solid lesson design principles. You'll find quite a few in this book, based on research and experience. I'm also betting you know that, just because something is *fun*, it may not be the best or most appropriate way to teach every lesson (that's the disclaimer). Use your best judgment and assess your students to make sure they're "getting it." Yes, I still regularly assess my students' progress. Even though I'm a big proponent of project-based learning, I'm a fan of assessment, too—when it's done right. I'm not afraid of testing because I know, if my class is engaging, students will be motivated to learn and retain more of what I teach. My hope is you'll feel the same confidence when you use the lesson plans and ideas you find in *Play Like a Pirate*. I promise, nearly every student will like these strategies more than a traditional sit-at-their-desk-for-an-hour lesson. As you consider developing your own playful teaching activities, keep these five guiding principles in mind:

1. **Make sure the fun applies to your content.** Sure, you can use a fun activity, but if your principal walks in—and he or she *will*, potentially at the worst possible moment—you want to be able to show that you're not "just playing." Be ready to explain how the activity connects to your content standards and/or your learning objective for the day. Personally, I believe there's value in "just playing"—to make connections and build rapport and camaraderie in your class. But your job is to bring students to a certain level of understanding and proficiency. If you can use these strategies to make your classroom more engaging while teaching the content, you're making your kids masters. Of the universe. Because they have the *powerrrrrrr*!!!! (I will neither explain nor apologize for that He-Man moment.)

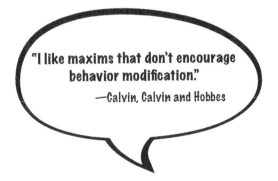

"I like maxims that don't encourage behavior modification."
—Calvin, Calvin and Hobbes

2. **Don't kill the fun.** While you're legitimizing the play, find ways to do it so students still enjoy the board game, action figure, the LEGO, or whatever it is. The content should be important, but you're using this particular activity to engage the students. *Engagement* in this case is *having fun.* If they're not having fun—if *you're* not having fun—you're missing the point of this book. Sometimes it can be stressful to set up the fun but, once you do so, let go of the stress. Bring the students back to the content a few times during the activity to explore what they're doing, the direction they're going, and why. Most of the time, they should be working (or *playing*—hopefully it's hard to tell the difference) independently of you and your *teachery* bossiness. On the flip side, you can take my approach: join in the activity alongside them. Being on the sidelines is boring. And, usually, if I think an activity is fun for them, it's fun for me, too. When I came up with my Mining board game (See page 88.), I sat down with the kids and got into it with them—trash talk included. Mostly they talked trash to me, but I got in a few zingers myself. I am a junior high teacher, after all!

3. **Make the activities versatile.** Each lesson idea presented in this book can be implemented in any classroom. One of the things I love about teaching seventh grade is that I'm able to take elementary or high school lesson plans and scale them up or down to meet my students' needs. Many of the lesson plans you'll find in *Play Like a Pirate* are taken directly from my classroom. When it comes down to it, middle school teachers have elementary-level learners in their classes, as well as kids who are nearly ready for college. When you take a bucket of LEGO bricks into any classroom, you're going to get kids on board, regardless of their age. What really matters is how you set up the activity, how you handle the content, and where you take the students afterwards. Like LEGO, design "toys," like TINKERTOY and

KAPLA® blocks, are extremely versatile. If you have access to a 3D printer or other twenty-first-century design and build tools, use them to create toys, inventions, or whatever else your students dream up. We live in an amazing time. Let's use it to push kids' creativity.

4. **Try out everything first.** Try out your activities on family members, friends (kids or adults), or colleagues before you bring them into your classroom. I've recruited family members to design action figures, friends to draw superheroes, and fellow teachers to play with LEGO bricks. Much of the time, I've been obsessive-compulsive enough to think ahead and avoid pitfalls, but we all have blind spots. Trying activities ahead of time helps you find those blind spots, so they don't derail your lesson. Plus, if your activity is fun for kids, hopefully the other people in your life will think it's fun, too. If not, they'll just make fun of you for years! At least, that's how *my* friends are. Jerks! I love them.

5. **Use toys you grew up with.** My lesson examples mainly use toys I loved as a kid, though some draw from toys that have become popular in more recent years. Use these examples and strategies, but also find some that use toys you loved. As much as I admire the whole My Little Pony thing—I just can't do it. But you Pony lovers? Share them. Gush about them. Your enthusiasm will be contagious and potentially embarrassing. If your face is a little flushed you know you've gushed enough to get people on board with you. Blushing is okay. To paraphrase *30 Rock*'s Liz Lemon, it means you've "gone to there."

RUBBER DUCKIE

As I mentioned earlier, *Sesame Street* had a profound impact on my childhood, shaping much of my view of the world. When I say childhood, I really mean my whole life. For my seventeenth birthday, my brother, Evan, gave me a little squeaky duck toy—because Ernie has his Rubber Duckie, and my brother thought I should have one, too. I loved it. Within a few years, Rubber Duckie (yes, that's also my duck's name) had been with me to Europe, California, Florida, Idaho—all the exotic places a boy from Utah wants to see when he grows up. In the era before selfies, Flat Stanley, or traveling garden gnomes, I took pictures of Rubber Duckie in all those distant lands, and his picture was better than one of me—he was always smiling in his!

Rubber Duckie turned twenty-five this year, and he's still my constant traveling companion. When I buy a new travel bag, it must have a "sidecar" pocket where he can ride and be easily accessed for pictures. Here's the thing: sharing this weird little hobby with my students builds a bond between them and me, and between them and my duck. (Sometimes they'd even bring me little rubber duckies as gifts.) When we talk about the Berlin Wall, I include a picture of Rubber Duckie at the Berlin Wall in my PowerPoint. Once they know I'd really been there, they ask me more questions than they would have if I had just shown them another image pulled off of Google. If you have a similar idiosyncrasy, use it. Maybe you collect spoons, rocks, or T-shirts when you travel. Sharing your collection will help students better relate to you and, hopefully, open their minds to broader worlds.

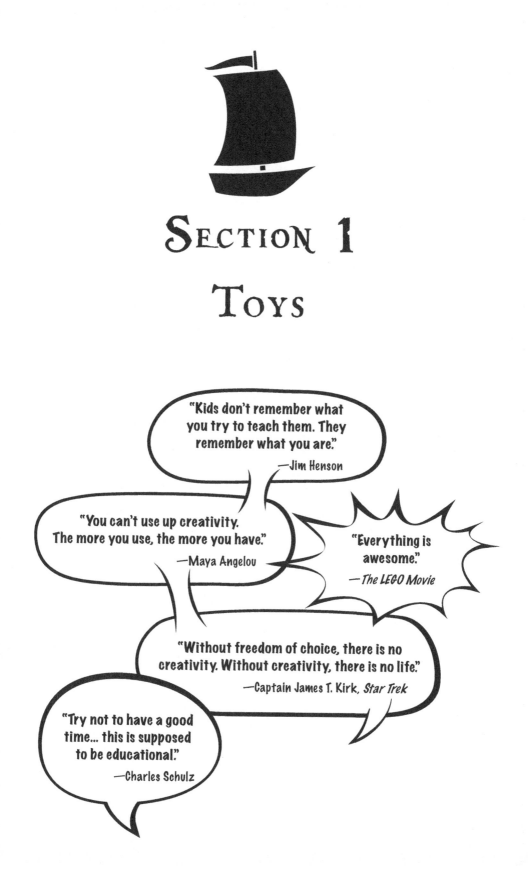

SECTION 1

TOYS

"Kids don't remember what you try to teach them. They remember what you are."
—Jim Henson

"You can't use up creativity. The more you use, the more you have."
—Maya Angelou

"Everything is awesome."
—*The LEGO Movie*

"Without freedom of choice, there is no creativity. Without creativity, there is no life."
—Captain James T. Kirk, *Star Trek*

"Try not to have a good time... this is supposed to be educational."
—Charles Schulz

HISTORY OF ACTION FIGURES

The history of action figures goes back to 1964, when Hasbro® created G.I. JOE "action figures" in a move to capitalize on the success of the Mattel® Barbie by having its own line of dolls for boys. Hasbro and Mego dominated this market through the 1970s, when the oil crisis necessitated a move from the 12" dolls to smaller figures. When Kenner introduced its *Star Wars* action figures in 1978, they were in a 3¾" scale, leading G.I. JOE to smaller-scale action figures. From that point on, most action figures have been made in a similar 3" to 5" size—easier to blow up with firecrackers (not that I ever did that) or strap them to bottle rockets. Holy moly! I'm that neighbor kid from *Toy Story*.

ACTION FIGURES

When the first *Star Wars* movie came out, I was just a pup—the perfect age for the toys, and while I didn't have all of them, between my neighbors and me, we had most of the main characters. In those days—before streaming, Blu-ray, DVD, or even VHS—playing with the action figures was one of the only ways we could relive the movie. I only saw it once in theaters and then waited for three years until *The Empire Strikes Back* came out, filling the gap with action figures and my imagination. Since then, I've collected various lines of action figures, including newer *Star Wars* toys and toys from *Star Trek*, *The Muppets*, Justice League, and Batman.

When I was in high school, I started "customizing" my own action figures—taking existing characters and switching out limbs, sculpting new heads, and painting them to be new characters. A little bit Frankensteiny, but it doesn't usually hurt anyone (except for the fumes). In college, I had the good fortune to help consult with Palisades Toys on action figures for *The Muppet Show*, *The X-Files*, and *Buffy the Vampire Slayer*. Examining fictional characters' biographies, skills, and possessions led me to create the strategy of using action figures in the classroom.

Action Figures in the Classroom

Kids don't play with action figures quite as much as they did in the 1980s, but there are still multiple aisles of them in every toy store. If you watch kids as they look at an action figure, whether it's Captain America, Darth Vader, or a Teenage Mutant Ninja Turtle, they all do the same thing. They pull it off the shelf, examine the front of the package, and look at the figure's details and the accessories it comes with. Then, they turn it over and scrutinize the back of the package. They read the short biography of the character and see images of playsets, vehicles, allies, and enemies—items they could buy (i.e., con their parents into buying) to complement that character. All of these elements are incorporated into my action-figure strategy.

As a teacher, my goal is for students to do research, evaluate the research, and share it with an audience. When they write biographies, I want them to summarize the life and accomplishments of a historic character into a few short paragraphs and make some connections to

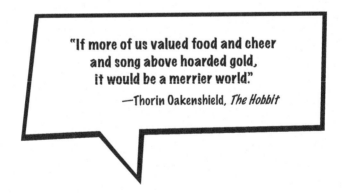

"If more of us valued food and cheer and song above hoarded gold, it would be a merrier world."
—Thorin Oakenshield, *The Hobbit*

other characters and their own lives. I also want them to have fun. And it's a bonus for me as teacher to be able to see, at a glance, whether the kid found and understood the essence of the person. If I can do that with one page instead of five pages of writing, I'm all for it. Even better, with this strategy, students design products they want to share with other students (and friends, parents, and siblings), instead of shoving them back into their folders or tossing them in the recycling bin. They also want to look at what other students have created. I don't know how often that happens with a traditional assignment, but I've seen it happen *every time* I've used the action-figure strategy.

The strategy is relatively simple because kids *get* it. Students create the "cardback" for an action figure—the piece of cardboard the action figure and its accessories are mounted on. Those key elements (biography, enemies, allies, etc.) are part of each cardback, and they're similar for each action figure. I want students to use this model to summarize their research on historical characters to prove to me that they understand the most pertinent things about their lives. To design an action figure well, they need a more comprehensive understanding of the character than they may get from a traditional biography.

Using the Template

FRONT

Main box. Students draw their character in full-body form, avoiding stick figures whenever possible. Younger students may need a dotted-line outline of a person to which they can add details. If the action figures represent real people, they should be as close as possible to the actual likeness, including things like facial features, hairstyle, and clothing. You could also think outside the box and have students design an action figure representing a more abstract idea—an element from the periodic table, a process, or one of the amendments to the Constitution.

Theme. Themes would be World War II, great astronomers or inventors, or characters from *Oliver Twist*. Any unit you're currently teaching can serve as the unifying theme for a line of action figures.

Portrait. Every action figure card has an image of the character as seen in the movie, comic book, cartoon, etc., which shows the buyer what the character "really" looks like. Ideally, the students should find an image—photograph, painting, or statue—of their historic characters. Images aren't typically available for literary characters, so students could draw their own. If you're tackling something more abstract, like an element from the periodic table or a geologic process, students could include a molecular diagram or a cross section of the process. Could a student figure out a way to represent a geometric shape or mathematical formula as an action figure? You bet!

Accessories. Accessories are the things characters hold, wear, or use, which set them apart from other characters in the same line. For example, Luke Skywalker always comes with a lightsaber because it's an essential part of his character. The lightsaber makes him complete. William Shakespeare might come with a quill pen, Benjamin Franklin with a kite, stove, bifocals, or almanac. (He was a busy guy.) What physical object would be essential to the character? How can these accessories help teach us about the person?

BACK

Biography. Students do the most writing on this section. I used to give an assignment that required students to research and present on a "Historic Hero." They could choose to do a traditional report, a poster, PowerPoint, or epic poem. Usually, I got twenty-three reports on Jackie Robinson—basically his Wikipedia page with a timeline. Part of that was my fault; part was the fault of the assignment itself. But I'd rather students be able to summarize the events of a person's life than just parrot back two pages they read online, which is where this action-figure biography comes into play. If done right, the summarization ensures greater depth of knowledge and, when combined with the other elements of the action figure, gives a more well-rounded view of the character's life.

Portrait. Another view of the character, either drawn by the student or printed from an online source, is included on the back of the card. Toys that are based on movies often use a still frame of the character from the movie—for example, Chris Evans as Captain America or Gal Gadot as Wonder Woman.

Playset. The playset is the environment the character lives in, works in, fights in, etc. It could also be a vehicle. For example, Thomas Jefferson's playset could be Monticello, Rosa Parks' a bus, and Sir Francis Drake's the *Golden Hind*. Playsets should help complete the character's biography. Some characters might have multiple playsets, and the more we know about the person, the better. The playset helps identify what part of the character's life the student is representing. For example, would the most important playset for Abraham Lincoln be a log cabin, the Illinois Statehouse, the White House, Gettysburg, or Ford's Theater? It depends on what part of his remarkable life the

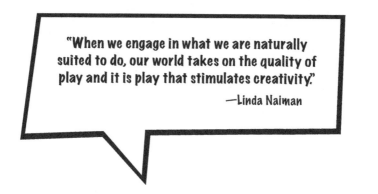

"When we engage in what we are naturally suited to do, our world takes on the quality of play and it is play that stimulates creativity."
—Linda Naiman

student has focused on. But I can tell you, if a middle school boy is reporting on Lincoln, it's going to be Ford's Theater.

If the assignment is to turn a mathematical formula into an action figure, students could use real-world applications of the formula, something I know I struggled with as a student. If you're tired of hearing students whine, "When am I ever going to use this in real life?!" have them find the "settings" in which the formula would be found.

If the student is designing an action figure representing an element from the periodic table, the "playset" would be compounds or materials where the element is found. If the element they're using is sodium, the playset could be table salt (sodium chloride) or bleach (sodium hypochlorite).

"Collect Them All." Here, students will include the other action figures in the same line, the ones that give us a more complete understanding of the character the student is designing. Just like you can't have Han Solo without Chewbacca, you can't have Alexander Hamilton without George Washington. In the case of biographies, I have students choose one character for each of the following:

- **An ally.** Students select a character from the same time period, fighting for the same cause, whether or not their character actually knew the person. For example, Christopher Columbus and Amerigo Vespucci were contemporaries and were both explorers. Even though they may not have known each other, well, I'd say they would qualify as allies.

- **An enemy.** Students choose a character from the same time period, but one acting against the goals of their character. For example, Governor George Wallace would be a great enemy of the Civil Rights Movement or Fidel Castro an enemy of JFK.

- **A modern ally.** Students choose a person living in the twenty-first century who is somehow carrying on the work of their character. While this may be difficult, it is also one of the most valuable pieces for helping students understand the past. When my nephew "guinea pigged" this strategy for me, he chose Galileo Galilei as his action figure and Stephen Hawking as the modern ally. Who would your students choose as a modern ally of Gandhi? Of Queen Elizabeth I? Of Ronald Reagan? Asking students to think about this opens up conversations with them and helps them make connections between their own lives and what they're studying.

POSSIBLE APPLICATIONS

Examples of Student Work

See the Big Picture. Some events in history were movements so large that you want students to understand more than just the "big names." Every kid knows Martin Luther King and Rosa Parks, but dozens of other Civil Rights Movement characters could be profiled. The same is true of leaders of the Civil War, ancient philosophers, scientists, or women's rights leaders. Using the action-figure strategy to highlight the many different aspects and characters that played a role in a historic event or movement helps them think and look beyond the most famous names of that time. If there are more than ten people you want your students to know, using this strategy helps them see there wasn't just one person in the event. It takes more than a single leader to shape history.

Thematic timeline. Find a theme with multiple variations over the course of your school year. For my history class, the idea of "revolution" worked nicely. I wanted students to understand what a revolution really is, not necessarily the details of every single revolution. So I'd look at political revolutions (French, American, communist), technological revolutions (bronze, industrial, Internet), or religious revolutions (Islam, Protestant) and have them design action figures based on those revolutions.

Long-term character biographies. Students pick different time periods of an important character's life. For example, they could choose George Washington as a child, during the French and Indian War, crossing the Delaware, at Valley Forge, in Philadelphia, at Mount Vernon, as president, and as a retired president. Characters selected would have to have distinct time periods worthy of study. Characters from epics like *The Odyssey* or *Les Misérables,* who live entire lifetimes in the pages of a book, are ideal for this project.

Astronomical phenomena. Students design action figures of planets, moons, stars, nebulae, pulsars, or asteroids. Their allies could be the astronomers who discovered them, accessories the probes, and missions exploring them.

Elements of the periodic table. Characters can be designed to represent the most common elements or the ones students find most interesting. Allies would be other elements they bond with most easily, and playsets would be the compounds where they're found.

Cell structures. Students could design figures for the nucleus, cytoplasm, ribosomes, mitochondria, or endoplasmic reticulum. But beyond the structure itself, students could include the functions of the structure and how it relates to the other cell systems.

Geographic features and processes. Plate tectonics, erosion, chemical weathering, sedimentation, subduction, volcanism, and earthquakes are all potential action figure models. Students could also include their impact on people and how they relate to or cause geologic features we see in the environment around us.

EXTENSIONS

Some teachers have taken the action-figure strategy even further, by starting students with the biography and action figure card and then having students actually create a figure. Figures have been made from paper dolls, salt clay, and aluminum foil. Some schools have the technology that allows students to print the 3D action figures they've designed. The makerspace movement is an amazing world for designers. It's just getting started in schools, and it's only going to get better.

Another extension of the action-figure strategy would be to have the students create a variant of their character's toy. A variant is made by taking an established character, often using the same sculpted mold, but changing the paint or accessories to make multiple versions of it. So a standard Batman figure could be dressed in white, given skis, and he's "Arctic Batman." Or give him some fins and a tank, and he's "Underwater Batman."

Historical action figure variants could be something like Susan B. Anthony as a ninja or FDR as a robot. Kids could make zombie, Bizarro, or gender-swapped variants. Once they've done the primary assignment, let them have some fun with it. If a kid just worked like

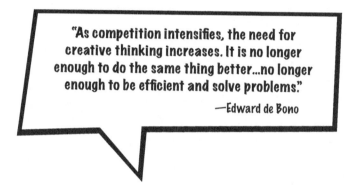

"As competition intensifies, the need for creative thinking increases. It is no longer enough to do the same thing better...no longer enough to be efficient and solve problems."

—Edward de Bono

crazy to learn about the women's suffrage movement and she needs to vent a little by "ninja-ing" up a Susan B., let her do it. You could require that the variant includes a historic fact or just let them go wild. Think back to when you were a kid. If you'd been able to "go crazy" after doing all the "legitimate" work, it may have saved some of your sanity.

Generally, I try to focus student biographies on the heroes of history. But kids (and adults) are fascinated by the great villains of history as well. If students can figure out a way to make a Mussolini action figure that doesn't celebrate the evils of fascism, I'm cool with that. But I always have them make a hero first.

DISPLAY STUDENT WORK

One of my favorite things about visiting elementary schools is seeing so much student art displayed. Almost every classroom has a vibrant, fun, and colorful gallery of artwork created by passionate student artists. It's too bad these galleries close down in middle school, where only the creations of art class students seem to merit attention. I want to encourage you to display what your kids have created. Students take pride in seeing their work in public, and they learn from other kids' creations as well. And while some teachers cover up students' names to preserve their anonymity, I believe that kids need to own and celebrate their work. Even older students enjoy seeing their work hung on the wall.

Some years, I have more than two hundred students in my classes daily. Every vertical surface in my classroom gets covered in student-drawn superheroes. I love it. The kids love it. Other teachers love it, too. Let's face it, *Play Like a Pirate* assignments are more fun (and sillier) than what your students are doing in other classes. Who gets excited about hanging essays up on the walls? Make your class safe and fun enough so students can celebrate their work.

HISTORY OF TRANSFORMERS

A subset of action figures, Transformers have managed to maintain popularity over the course of three decades—and counting. Autobots and Decepticons are robots that transform into cars, planes, dinosaurs, spaceships, animals, and more. In fact, there's probably been a Transformer made to take almost any form imaginable—except my 1992 Geo Metro, which would have been awesome!

TRANSFORMERS

As a kid, I loved watching the *Transformers* cartoon but, since all my toy "eggs" were committed to the *Star Wars* basket, I didn't have any of the toys. I loved drawing them, though. I remember one time drawing Transformers on some pieces of lumber that my dad had left over from a project. I cut the wood into shorter lengths and used pencils and crayons to draw robots on one side of each piece and the vehicles on the other. I laid them down to play with the "cars," and then did my best impression of the *metal-on-metal-clanking-transforming* sound, and, like magic (I stood the pieces of wood on end), they became robots! Sounds kind of sweet—and sad—doesn't it?

TRANSFORMING THE
TRADITIONAL EDUCATION

The template for Transformers packaging is slightly different from the template of a traditional action figure: the robot version of the character is pictured as well as the object it transforms into, which is usually a vehicle. Including a vehicle in the student project can be fun, even if the character is from a bygone era. What would Harriet Tubman

Examples of Student Work

transform into? A train? A subway? A submarine? You could make a case for any of those in my classroom. As long as the student can justify his choice, he can choose any form he wants. Of course, the robot version of the character could transform into other things. For example, is Harry S. Truman best represented by an atomic bomb, a plane used in the Berlin Airlift, or the United Nations? Would Andrew Jackson be a bulldozer, pushing Native American tribes off their land, or a railroad representing Jacksonian democracy? The robot could have features of the real person's appearance (i.e., Teddy Roosevelt's mustache or Amelia Earhart's flight helmet), as well as features of what the character transforms into.

As with traditional action figures, this Transformers strategy can be used outside of history and social studies. For example, what would a robot version of Jupiter look like? What would it transform into? What about the robot version of the mathematical concept of pi? Pushing students to think creatively about what they're studying is the goal. Instead of filling in blanks on a worksheet, they're thinking outside the box, considering the application of their knowledge.

The other consistent feature of Transformers packaging is a bar graph representing the character's strengths and weaknesses. For example, Optimus Prime outranks all characters in leadership skills (He *is* Optimus Prime after all!) but has slower speed than several other Autobots who transform into sports cars and less physical strength than some other much larger robots. For historic and literary characters, encourage students to include physical strengths but also strengths of intelligence, courage, and kindness. And insist students add a unique character trait to their Transformers—a quality that makes them memorable for doing something different than their contemporaries.

STUDENTS AND ART

Most kids like to draw. They color, they doodle, and they sketch. But around fifth grade, something happens to make these kids stop drawing. They realize they don't have the artistic skills their peers have or, horribly, an adult in their lives tells them they don't have those skills or that pursuing art is a waste of time. At that point, students start apologizing for their drawings and saying, "I can't draw." And with art classes taking the back burner to tested subjects, I'm afraid even more students will get that message.

One of my core beliefs is that every child—and every adult—can be an artist. So, my goal is to encourage every student to draw to the best of his or her ability. And yes, I've banned stick figures from my classroom (I tell my students that a stick figure killed my twin brother). But in exchange for banning stick figures, I give them a template or a quick sketch they can use as a scaffold. Give your students the tools they need to succeed.

> "Every artist dips his brush in his own soul and paints his own nature into his pictures."
> —Henry Ward Beecher

HISTORY OF HOT WHEELS

Elliot Handler, co-founder of Mattel, saw the success of the British Matchbox cars and decided to launch his own line of die-cast toy cars. From its first series of sixteen cars released in 1968, Hot Wheels grew into the dominant line of toy cars in the United States. Offering a mix of real-world cars and fantasy cars, Hot Wheels is a perennial brand kids have grown up with. Hot Wheels customizable, orange race tracks have long been a staple of many play rooms. How many ten-year-olds have spent countless hours reconfiguring their tracks so their cars would loop and jump and make a cool landing—on their sleeping cats?

Hot Wheels

I grew up in the 1970s—an era of iconic cartoon vehicles: *Scooby-Doo*'s Mystery Machine, the sputtering *Speed Buggy*, George Jetson's space car, the Japanese *Speed Racer*, and Fred Flintstone's foot-powered family ride. The 1970s and 1980s also gave us several small-screen, live-action, iconic vehicles: *Knight Rider*'s K.I.T.T., Bo and Luke Duke's General Lee, or *The A-Team*'s simple-but-distinctive GMC van. On the big screen, cars got even more bizarre but were grounded in real-world vehicles: *Back to the Future*'s DeLorean time machine or the *Ghostbusters*' ECTO-1. However, all of these cars—no matter how amazing they were—could be trumped with one word: Batmobile. Of course, Batman has the unfair advantage of a billionaire's budget, so he always rides in style. If you're looking at iconic cars, the Batmobile is always going to be the one to beat.

Hot Wheels: Design Your Own Car

Because so many students (and teachers) love cars, using lessons with a Hot Wheels template can be a cool way to engage them in learning. One way to do so is to have students design cars representing themselves and use those cars to track their progress through a unit or quarter. I vividly remember using a spaceship chart in elementary school to track the multiplication tables I was learning. While it did push me to memorize them, if I had been given the latitude to design my own spaceship, I would've been even more motivated. Change those spaceships into cars racing around an elaborate *Mario Kart*-style track, and you've created an exciting way for students to track their progress!

Designing a car can be difficult for elementary kids, but there are some great picture books to use as resources. My favorite is *If I Built a Car* by Chris Van Dusen, which encourages a kid's imagination—and yours too—to run wild. If a kid wants to fill her car with water and make it an "aquarium mobile," let her do it—it's her car!

In recent years, Hot Wheels has moved beyond cars you see on the street and even beyond pop-culture cars, like the Batmobile and the Mystery Machine. Today you can find Hot Wheels cars stylized to represent superheroes, Jedi, Muppets, and *Looney Tunes'* characters. Superman is represented by a blue sports car with a red "extreme spoiler" that stretches out behind the car like a cape. Darth Vader is a sleek black car with a triangular grill, domed windshield, and red lightsaber side panels. Showing students these examples can inspire them to embrace designing their own car. Any number of defining characteristics can be used:

Examples of Student Work

34

GEOGRAPHY
- Characteristics of a particular country
- Landforms
- Geographic processes

SOCIAL STUDIES
- World leaders
- Political systems
- Philosophies

HEALTH
- Bones
- Organs
- Systems

ENGLISH LANGUAGE ARTS
- Characters in a novel
- Punctuation
- Parts of speech

SCIENCE
- Elements
- Cell structures

SPEEDOMETRY™

Like LEGO and Minecraft, Hot Wheels has recently developed its own education initiative. Hot Wheels Speedometry is a series of lesson plans using cars, race tracks, gravity clamps, and loops. The free lesson plans are STEM-focused, with the bulk of the content about potential and kinetic energy, force, gravity, and friction. The program is being piloted in the United States with fourth-grade classrooms in 2015 and 2016 and will hopefully grow from there. Hot Wheels are great toys, and I'm excited to see an official program using them as educational tools.

EXTENSIONS

SELL IT!

One extension activity with Hot Wheels is to have students write a commercial advertising the car they've designed. What features would attract a buyer? How does their vehicle meet the standards of the unit you're assessing? Having them write a concise description in the form of an ad is another way to gauge their understanding and help them learn to summarize.

DESIGN YOUR OWN TRACK

Another idea is to have kids design their own tracks. Manipulating the flexible orange track into loops, curves, and jumps is one of the best things to do with Hot Wheels. Your sedate little cars suddenly transform into truly dynamic toys—sometimes even projectiles, depending on how many cats are in your room (the more cats, the more rocketing cars!).

What if your students took this Hot Wheels-style track model and used it to illustrate the timeline of historic events or a sequence of developments in a novel? Students make timelines for all sorts of lessons. Timelines are good and important, but conventional timelines can be static. In this model, the car can represent an individual character, a country, or a broader view of the events. The car starts on tracks at a high elevation, causing it to accelerate enough to propel it through the rest of the track. The protagonist in a novel does the same thing. What sparks a revolution, a war, or an invention? Where does the character get thrown into a loop, or have to jump over a gap, or even completely fly off the tracks? Does the track split and then come back together? Kids have grown up playing with these tracks; they understand how they work and can use the pieces to bring any topic to life.

Hot Wheels track is cheap. It comes in dozens of different shapes and sizes, with connectors to make loops, jumps, and banks. Find ways to use it. Students will remember a tangible *Crime and Punishment* Raskolnikov Hot Wheels track timeline better than they'll remember a written one. Label the events of the novel on the track, then let Raskolnikov fly! Where does his story begin, where does it end, and

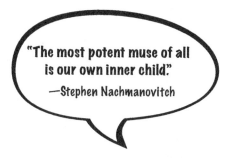

"The most potent muse of all is our own inner child."

—Stephen Nachmanovitch

where does he fly off the track? Are there choices he could have made along the way, or is his path as one-way as the Hot Wheels track is? I'm sure Dostoyevsky had Hot Wheels track in mind when he wrote the book. He'll be delighted his idea didn't die with him.

"TRACK" YOUR RESEARCH

In a science class, students could use the Hot Wheels track to delineate the parts of the scientific method: begin with the question, conduct background research, construct the hypothesis, perform the experiment, etc. The Hot Wheels track could even *be* the experiment—using variables in the height and length of the track, the size and weight of the car, or the desired distance. There are myriad ways to adapt this relatively simple, inexpensive piece of equipment for classroom use.

Could these track designs be done on paper? Of course. But kids will remember them more if they actually get to build and execute the track. Whether they work solo, with a partner, or in teams, they should be able to explain why they've designed the track the way they have and how it represents the content or concept you're working on.

SECRET SOCKS

My menu of idiosyncrasies now includes Secret Socks. I outgrew the cartoony neckties which were a staple of my classroom wardrobe—several *Sesame Street* ties, including one Kermit the Frog tie I wore with matching Adidas Kermit shoes, but only to weddings and funerals. While the ties fit my personality and I still wear them on occasion, I didn't want to wear them as often to school. So I started wearing interesting socks instead. I've got Darth Vader socks and *Doctor Who* socks. Socks featuring Superman, Green Lantern, Voltron—nearly every other member of the Justice League—even a pair with Batman on one sock and Robin on the other. And not to be outdone by DC, Marvel icons also live in my sock collection: Captain America, Iron Man, and others. Pop culture icons? I've got them—socks with pigeons and sharks—I even have hashtag socks that say *#SOCK* (no kidding).

They're "Secret" Socks because no one has to know I'm wearing them. I can have a meeting with parents or a principal, with the governor—with an emperor penguin—and they won't dismiss what I'm saying because I'm wearing a silly tie. Plus, students respect me. They see me every day and know there's more to me than a silly tie. My Secret Socks allow me— especially on more serious occasions—some degree of dignity. But not too much. In fact, every time I wear a new pair of Secret Socks, I tweet and post a picture to Instagram with *#SecretSocks* or *#SecretSocksoftheDay*. Kind of obviates the secrecy, but that's what I love about it: it's a secret, but everyone can share it.

HISTORY OF BARBIE

Barbie, like Hot Wheels, was another creation of Mattel founders, Ruth and Elliot Handler. Groundbreaking for her departure from baby and toddler dolls, Barbie has been around since 1959. Despite everything written about Barbie—her modeling unrealistic expectations, negative impact on body image, and the "Math is hard!" Barbie—she's still a favorite. Kids still want to play with Barbie dolls. Do they represent future dreams? Conspicuous consumption? A tide of pink plastic which may eventually overwhelm us? Maybe. But kids know Barbie, and they know Ken. They know their awkward and ambiguous relationship, and we can take advantage of that.

BARBIE

As a kid, I didn't have Barbies, but my older sister did. Although I was expressly forbidden to touch them, my *Star Wars* action figures sometimes visited Barbie's condo tower while my sister was out of sight. My dad built the four-story condo tower, and since my action figures were one-third the height of my sister's Barbies, it was a great base for them to hide out. And it had electric lighting. Maybe flush toilets too; I don't remember. In any case, I know Barbie and have my own fond memories of her. And I'll bet the girls and boys in your class do, too. Put those memories to work by letting Barbie help your students see your content from her perspective.

Here's what I mean: history is often presented as the history of white men. Dead, white men. Rich, dead, white men. When women are mentioned, it's often as an aside or as the one really great woman of a particular era. Sure, Abigail Adams was amazing, as was Joan of Arc and Rosa Parks, but there were other remarkable women our students can learn about. Use Barbie to put the spotlight on some of the lesser-known female history makers.

BARBIE: TIME TRAVELER, RENAISSANCE WOMAN

Some history-based strategies using Barbie write themselves. For example, since Barbie hit the toy aisle, she has depicted women's roles, careers, and fashion. As you study different periods of history, use images of historic Barbies and have students pick ten they think best represent a particular era or theme.

Certain history lessons traditionally use women as a lens to examine an entire society. One of the best examples is the comparison and contrast between the Spartans and Athenians. Use Barbie to help teach how the roles of women in those two neighboring city-states were profoundly different. A Spartan Barbie would be a different design and have different accessories from an Athenian Barbie.

Examples of Student Work

You could do the same with nearly any historic period or conflict: North versus South in the American Civil War, czarinas versus serfs, flappers versus temperance crusaders, and Okies versus Wall Street.

In addition to comparing women living in the same place or time, you can also compare and contrast women across wider regions. The roles of women in ancient China were vastly different from those in ancient India, for example. Have students compare the life of a "typical" American woman today with that of a woman from Afghanistan or Kenya. Or you could span across time periods, contrasting women from the twenty-first century with women from any other historic period.

In my opinion, the best way to teach about women's history is alongside and integrated into all of history. That said, sometimes it's good to step back and view women's history as a separate timeline, pulling out and emphasizing individuals and their contributions. We do this with historic male characters all the time, so why not create women-only timelines? Using Barbie for this probably sets me up to be burned in effigy by some of my women's history colleagues, but I'm saying it anyway. Barbie's a good fit for this purpose. (And yeah, Eleanor Roosevelt would make a great Barbie doll.) Challenge your students to use Barbie to depict the most important women from each decade of American history. Can they distill the achievements of an entire generation into a single personality? Who would they choose, and could they justify their answers? This activity would take research and some thought, but they'd have fun with it.

Over the years, Barbie has held various careers, modeling those as potential opportunities for young girls, but even as recently as 2014, Mattel was still issuing merchandise that implied girls weren't as good as men in software engineering and programming careers. Ask your students to evaluate Barbie's careers: astronaut, chef, martial arts instructor, etc. What hasn't she been? What could she be?

For the past fifty-seven years, when we thought of Barbie, most of us automatically pictured a leggy, tan, unrealistically proportioned, blonde American. And for Mattel, that became a problem—one that negatively affected sales. Yes, there have been Barbies representing other races since 1980, but they all flaunted the same "perfect" bodies—until now.

Barbie Timeline Gallery

In January 2016, Mattel announced a major change. Instead of making every Barbie body from the same mold, now four different body types are available. Classic Barbie isn't going anywhere, but now she's joined by "petite," "curvy," and "tall" Barbies In addition to the new body sizes and shapes, the dolls come in seven new skin tones and with a variety eye colors and hair textures and colors.

This transition is as much in response to Mattel's slumping sales as it is to any sort of new forward-thinking agenda. Yes, it might be healthier for children to see a wider range of body types in their toys, but Mattel's leadership also recognized that Barbie had to evolve if the company was going to regain market share lost to LEGO and other toymakers.

In the coming months and years, it may well be that the Barbies in our students' Dream Houses will look more like our students and the women they see around them every day. And that's a good thing.

Barbie is well known for her accessories, and while it's probably a negative message to send kids, Barbie's "stuff" is an inherent part of her image. The Barbie Dream House is the ultimate expression of that and, like the dolls themselves, can be used to demonstrate how the American Dream has changed over time. The Dream House of the 1970s is not the Dream House of the 2010s.

Have students change the time period of the Dream House and make a Great Depression Dream House or an Industrial Revolution Dream House. From this activity, they could springboard into other problem-solving activities. For example, how could they adapt the current Dream House to fit a different climate? Or you could change the geographic location *and* time period and have students create a Medieval China Dream House, Roman Villa Dream House, or an Inuit Dream House.

MUSIC

Music isn't one of my natural, go-to teaching strategies. In fact, I don't listen to music on my own very often (I'm an NPR/audiobook/podcast kind of guy). The music I do listen to is whatever my wife and kids are listening to; thankfully, they keep me somewhat up-to-date on new songs. But music in the classroom? Nope, never used it. When I hear about teachers having a classroom playlist that includes *The Beatles*, my mind focuses on Beatles' facts. Rather than recalling melodies, I think "Ah. Yes. The. Beatles. John. Paul. George. Ringo. 1964. Ed. Sullivan. Yoko." No, I don't get music. But students do. So after going to one too many conferences where other history teachers raved about using music with kids, I decided to give it a try. My Great Depression unit was coming up, so I picked out three songs from the *O Brother, Where Art Thou?* soundtrack, which were actually written in the 1930s. I printed the lyrics for the students and added them to my PowerPoint. But then what? I wasn't sure what to do. Of course, we'd listen to the songs and analyze the lyrics, but then what? I wanted to do more than that. So…we sang along! You need to understand that, although I can *sing*, I'm not a *singer*. But I sang. And I coaxed and cajoled every class—every kid—into singing with me. I played the air banjo and we sang super loud (We had to apologize to the teacher next door for shaking things off the walls.). And I loved it! The kids loved it! I was hooked and started looking for other songs to include in "Hobo Day." I added a "Hippie Day," including protest songs from the 1960s and dressed up like a hippie that day. The teacher I'd apologized to even brought me a tambourine to use. The following year, I added labor organizer Joe Hill's songs and World War I songs. At some point kids would say, "Mr. Rollins. Ugh. This isn't a music class." And they were right. But it was a class where we *celebrated* music.

HISTORY OF PLAY-DOH

Did you know Play-Doh was originally a wallpaper cleaner? Pretty amazing, considering how much time adults spend cleaning Play-Doh off of (and out of!) tables, carpets, and couches! Now you do. Maybe that fun toy fact will save you on *Jeopardy!* someday. Play-Doh made the move from work to fun when a teacher told inventor Joe McVicker that traditional modeling clay was hard for her students to use. McVicker shipped some of his very malleable wallpaper cleaner to schools for students to use. Students loved it, and by 1957, Play-Doh in primary colors was on store shelves. By the time I was a kid, it was available in dozens of colors. Now it comes in every color and glitter and glow-in-the-dark option imaginable!

PLAY-DOH

I love Play-Doh—the colors, the feel, and that smell. I love that smell! Play-Doh and Crayola Crayons are two childhood smells that immediately evoke memories—good memories! Even the time I ate some Play-Doh (surprisingly soapy tasting—I don't recommend it) ended up being a good memory. Thank goodness it's non-toxic.

Some teachers use Play-Doh, salt clay, and modeling clay interchangeably, but they're actually not the same. Modeling clay, Sculpey® Modeling Compound for example, is great, but initially it is harder to work with than the other two types. It takes some kneading and warming up before you can really do anything with it. On the upside, you can bake your modeling clay sculptures in an oven to create something permanent. Salt clay is stickier but hardens over time in the open air, giving you a more permanent piece than Play-Doh does. Instead of making homemade salt clay, you can also purchase "air dry" modeling clay in most craft stores, and it often comes in larger containers or bulk quantities compared to the little cans of Play-Doh.

Sometimes, though, you want actual Play-Doh. Play-Doh is wonderful for classroom use because, if kept it in its airtight containers, it stays malleable for a long time. Plus, it comes in vibrant, distinct colors and is affordable. Additionally, there are hundreds of relatively inex-

"Adventure is out there."
—Ellie Fredricksen, *Up*

pensive molds and factory-style pressing devices available. Whether you want to extrude spaghetti, make a star, or mold pieces of buildings, you can find a device to do it. Another great aspect of Play-Doh is the complete lack of a learning curve; students instinctively know how to play with Play-Doh. Because that's true, when you plan on giving students chunks of Play-Doh to use in class, you need to be prepared to give them at least five minutes of "free play" as a warm-up to your "real" classroom activity.

Using Play-Doh in Class

One outcome of technology is the shift in our economy from making and buying handmade, artisan products to producing and selling factory-made items. To highlight the implications of that shift, I divide my students into two groups and give them Play-Doh as a medium. One group receives an exemplar of a star ornament—handmade and with an elaborate crosshatched pattern. Their assignment is to make stars of the same size but with whatever elaborate details they want. Their only specific instruction is that their stars should be beautiful.

The other group of students forms an assembly line and is given star cookie-cutter templates and rolling pins. Their assignment is to make as many stars as they can in the allotted time.

We can draw a lot of lessons from this activity: Which group can make more stars, faster and more uniformly? As a consumer, would you rather buy the handmade, beautiful stars or the multiple, uniform stars? As a store owner, which type would you rather put on your shelves? Can there be value to the homemade version? Would the handmade stars be more or less expensive than the mass-produced ones? When is having uniform products a good thing?

Feel free to use multiple prompts in one class period when using Play-Doh. One of the great pleasures of Play-Doh is making something, destroying it, and then making something completely different. Encourage your students to make an object, smash it, and then pass that color of Play-Doh to the next kid. I also love using Play-Doh in small groups—not necessarily in collaboration but in situations where students can work on their own objects while also seeing what their peers are making. When the medium is so easy to work with, students seem to focus more on enjoying others' work than competing as "artists." Finally, don't hesitate to mix in some absurd creations with the actual curriculum-based sculpting projects. Play-Doh is quick and easy. Have fun with it!

**Examples of
Student Work**

Play-Doh Prompts

Of the endless ways to use Play-Doh, here are several prompts to consider:

- Expectations for the new school year
- Characteristics of your personality
- What you wish your teacher knew about you
- Best childhood memory
- Favorite school subject
- Classroom rules you should have
- Emotions
- Bullying
- Your school mascot
- Artifacts from a civilization you're studying
- State symbols
- National symbols
- Geographic landforms
- Maps showing topography and other geographic features
- Busts of historic figures
- New monuments for your community
- Organs of the body
- Cell structures
- Types of rock
- Chemical compounds
- Plot points in a story
- Mathematical relationships and equations
- Fractions and ratios
- Abstract ideas without using "shortcuts" (for example, illustrating peace without using a peace symbol or love without using a heart shape, etc.)

You can extend these prompts by having students create short, museum-style labels and explanatory paragraphs, or adding detail to their sculptures. For example, could students add texture to their Play-Doh body organs to indicate their function? Could they add details to their chemical compounds to illustrate what they look like in "real life"? Personally, I usually have a "no-mixing-colors" policy with Play-Doh, so colors remain true. But in cases where you want students to have more options and more detail to demonstrate their understanding, allowing mixing for multiple colors is helpful.

STOP-MOTION ANIMATION

Gumby knew it. Mr. Bill knew it. Your kids know it. Play-Doh is the perfect medium for stop-motion animation. iMovie and Flipbook are the best known apps for students to create stop-motion animation, but there are probably a dozen more. If your students are working on a project that includes a process or change over time, visually incorporating the idea would be fun. Yes, it takes some time but, whether they're studying the water cycle, changing demographics, or territorial expansion, students will definitely remember anything they've learned by using Play-Doh and creating a short animated video.

SCHOOL SPIRIT

Most schools have some kind of Spirit Week, when the hallways are decorated with posters announcing "Monday is Pajama Day!" or "Tuesday is Beach Day!" or "Wednesday is Dress Like Your Favorite Teacher (and it better be flattering if you want to earn 'brownie points') Day!" Most of the time, teachers don't participate. They believe that Spirit Week is for kids, not teachers, and spend the week irritated by the annual interruption. Of course, there are notable exceptions: that teacher who participates a little too hard. Yeah, I may be one of those, celebrating Pajama Day by wearing my Kermit the Frog slippers with my *Sesame Street* bathrobe, complete with bedhead, sleep mask, and even eating cereal in class. On Beach Day, I wear a kid's size inflatable Big Bird swim ring squeezed around my not-so-kid-size torso and wait all day to see if it will burst. Thankfully, it hasn't yet, but I've had a few close calls—hearing the squeaky sound of plastic stretched almost to the point of *kaboom*! Don't get me wrong. I'm not saying you need to *be* "that" teacher, but it's definitely more fun—for the kids *and* you—if you are. And I assure you—any credibility you might lose with students because of your attire will be surpassed by their excitement and approval of what a freak you are!

HISTORY OF THE SMURFS

The Smurfs are the creations of the Belgian artist Pierre Culliford, known as Peyo. Beginning in 1958, they enchanted European comic book readers with their blueness, hats, mushroom houses, berry-based economy, and anti-Gargamel (their human nemesis) political platform. In 1981, the Smurfs jumped across the pond and into a Hanna-Barbera cartoon series. Led by Papa Smurf, the community of about one hundred Smurfs, including one Smurfette, lived in a village in the enchanted forest. Each episode focused on a handful of characters, many of whom were named for their occupations (Baker, Poet, Painter). Others were named for an overwhelming personality trait (Jokey, Clumsy, and Brainy, who could've alternatively been known as Annoying Smurf). *The Smurfs* made it to onto the big screen in a series of forgettable movies beginning in 2011.

THE SMURFS

T he Smurfs were a Saturday morning cartoon staple for me, even though I didn't have any of their toys. In fact, their design and mass numbers made them a part of everyone's childhood in the 1980s. The cartoon's simple stories were safe for kids but still had a sense of adventure. They were also just darn cute. I had a few friends in elementary school who called my little brother "Smurf," and while he might not like it today, at the time, it was a clear term of endearment. I mean, he's not even blue.

Most of the strategies in this book—and most of history for that matter—focus on the biography of a single individual. Even if a lesson relates to a larger historical movement, it's often focused on the role of one extraordinary individual from the era. This singular focus helps students find role models and strive to *be* extraordinary.

However, sometimes it's valuable to step back and look at the bigger picture. To do that, it's sometimes useful to examine the roles of the many and diverse individuals who comprise a collective group. The Smurfs offer a great tool for looking at social studies topics related to community building. For example, what roles are in historic communities? How are those roles filled? How has it changed over time?

There are also bigger ideas of "community." For example, biomes are communities. Animal and plant families (okay, maybe a genus) are communities. Sections of the orchestra are communities. Consider political movements, branches of government, and organs of the body (even though they are probably more like villages than communities). The same strategy can be applied to understand how they work.

A Smurfy Classroom Strategy

The Smurf Village had one hundred Smurfs, but for simplicity, my template has six generic Smurfs, Papa Smurf, and one Smurfette. My lessons often focus on the leader of a community, the president, or monarch of a nation, for example. On the template, Papa Smurf is the leader and is set apart from the others. Smurfette represents the role of women, and the six other Smurfs would be the most urgent needs for the community. Remembering Smurfs are usually named for their occupation, they can be labeled accordingly on the template or their hats customized, adding small details to differentiate them from each other. You might ask students who (or what) would be necessary for the community to succeed, and how would students define *success*? Jamestown and some other historic communities initially had only a minimum number of women—and they failed. What could this say about the importance of women to the success of a community?

I have another template that flips the traditional Smurf Village—ninety-nine Smurfettes and only one male—to help students think through community-related issues. How would this change make society different? In what ways might it be better, worse, or just different? What if the community was a matriarchal society led by *Mama Smurf*, but everything else remained the same? What if the Smurf Village more accurately mirrored the real world with a 50/50 balance between female and male? Is there a problem if Smurfette replaces Handy Smurf?

How could this relate to non-human "societies," such as the roles of different bees in a hive? The queen bee runs the show, but without the efforts of the drones and the workers, the hive would quickly collapse. Each bee needs to fulfill its role in order for the community to be successful, and those roles are all interconnected. The same could be said for different organelles within a cell or even the different stages of the water cycle. Each is part of a community (or communal process) that can't be successful without multiple parts.

I'm a fan of using urban planning to problem solve. Challenge students to invent a community they believe would solve the problems that they see around them. Then ask them to compare and contrast their invented community with their own community or with an *ideal* community. What changes would be needed to make their community ideal? How can students be a part of or help create that ideal community?

**Examples of
Student Work**

SHARE YOUR FAILURES

Students (and their parents) are bothered when we teachers act like we're perfect, as if any and every problem in the classroom is a student's fault, not ours. We seem to think we must always be *right*. Maybe that's one reason we sometimes fear trying new things. New technology is scary because if it fails in front of the class, we'll look like fools. But I think it's okay—even healthy—to share some of your mistakes and failures. I tell my students I really struggled with math in the seventh grade. It's still a weak spot for me. For anything too far past counting mittens or dividing a pie into slices, I start to panic. When teaching something I don't particularly like because it was hard for me to learn, I tell my students what my misconceptions were and how I learned the material despite them. The most spectacular example of my own imperfection came from my time as a contestant on *Who Wants To Be a Millionaire*. Want to be a millionaire? Know about Walt Whitman! I used all three of my "lifelines" trying to answer a question about him. I eventually chose the right answer, thanks to my sister, but ended up taking home $8,000 instead of $1 million. (And there are so many more zeroes in a million! *Sigh*.) Anyway, I share my *Millionaire* experience with my students to show them we can't know everything. We don't need to know everything. But we do need to be aware of and learn from our failures. Failing isn't bad because (most of the time) it isn't permanent. Learn. Change. Grow. And let your students watch you!

> " To live a creative life, we must lose our fear of being wrong."
> —Joseph Chilton Pearce

HISTORY OF LEGO

The LEGO Group was founded in 1932 by Ole Kirk Kristiansen. The name *LEGO* comes from the Danish *leg godt* meaning "play well." For many years, LEGO focused on wooden toys, and they introduced the plastic LEGO bricks we now know and love in 1958. However, it actually took decades for it to evolve into the LEGO I know personally. For example, 1978 brought us the first minifigures with movable arms and legs (and the adorable little yellow smiley faces which still make me happy). In addition to minifigures, 1978 also brought the first distinct Town, Space, and Castle themes. As of 2015, The LEGO Group is the largest toy company in the world, nosing ahead of Mattel and Hasbro—an amazing achievement when you consider the simplicity of the LEGO toy!

LEGO

I didn't actually have any LEGO sets until I was about twelve years old. After *Return of the Jedi* in 1983, those action figures petered out, and I needed a new toy fix. Enter my grandma, who gave me a LEGO tow truck. (Thinking back, she probably intended it for my younger brother, but since we played together pretty well and I was on the level of a six-year-old when it came to toys, we both enjoyed it.) For several years I received LEGO sets as gifts and occasionally bought them for myself through my teen years, until 1999 when LEGO got the *Star Wars* license and my Dark Ages were over. For good! From that point, I was buying LEGO for myself and my sons, with the tacit understanding that once they stopped playing with it, it would revert back to the original purchaser. I even became an official Adult Fan of LEGO (AFOL). Obsession may not equal happiness, but it's a lot of fun!

EASING LEGO INTO YOUR CLASSROOM

While there are plenty of ways to bring LEGO into your classroom, the simplest is doing a quick search for ideas on Flickr, Google Images, or other photo sites. For example, search "World War I LEGO" and you'll find biplanes, trench warfare, battleships, and tanks—all built on a small scale and surprisingly accurate historically. These images don't include (much) blood, and seeing LEGO minifigures fighting the War to End All Wars is somehow both innocent and morbid. Embed those images into your classroom on a poster, slide show, or as a photo analysis exercise. How did the builder accurately depict details? Where did the builder go wrong? LEGO can be fun even when not used hands-on. Certain blogs specialize in hosting the best LEGO builds. The best of these is Brothers Brick (http://www.brothers-brick.com). If you want to narrow your Internet search, this is a good place to start. Nearly every major historic event has been built and rebuilt using LEGO, and images of these have been posted online by the obsessed LEGO fans who created them. Use them.

Some LEGO projects take a larger view. For example, in his *50 States of LEGO* project, Jeff Friesen built small vignettes to represent each of the fifty states. What a great jumping-off project for research on the states! Instruct students to look at the image, investigate why Mr. Friesen chose a particular scene to represent a certain state, critique the image, and create an alternate image to represent that state. Friesen also has a similar project for the provinces of Canada.

Another potential project uses LEGO's official architecture line, where iconic buildings from around the world have been translated into miniature models. The current architecture collection comprises nearly two dozen buildings and structures, including masterpieces by Frank Lloyd Wright, iconic skyscrapers like the Empire State Building and Willis Tower, and cultural landmarks like Big Ben and the Sydney Opera House. Students can analyze which cultures are underrepresented and come up with proposals to add another building to the Architecture line. The LEGO Architecture website includes rationales for why certain buildings are picked and why others are not. Students can develop counterarguments to get their building included in the lineup.

In addition to LEGO's own extensive publishing lineup, dozens of books from various authors and publishers highlight the possibilities of using LEGO. Some of my favorites include Warren Elsmore's books *Brick Wonders: Ancient, Modern, and Natural Landmarks in LEGO* and *Brick City: LEGO for Grownups*. Nathan Sawaya uses LEGO as a medium to create art. No Starch Books has a collection of titles about architecture, art—even one about medieval English history—using LEGO as illustrations. Any of these can inspire you and your students to create projects for your classroom.

My goal is to engage students while they put their ideas into a format I can understand. With LEGO, they can, by doing the design work on paper *and* building with LEGO bricks and pieces.

LEGO Architecture

Quick Glossary

Because kids are generally familiar with LEGO, I recommend you also familiarize yourself with the principles and special vocabulary of LEGO before turning students loose on a design project. Otherwise, when your students ask you about "studs," things could get weird fast.

Bricks—The thicker LEGO pieces resembling, well…bricks.

Minifigure—Debuting in 1978, these are the little LEGO dudes (and dudettes) included with most LEGO sets.

Plates—The thinner LEGO pieces. Three plates stacked on top of each other equal the height of one LEGO brick.

Set—An individual LEGO playset kit, complete with instructions, pieces, and minifigures. A castle playset could include the actual castle along with a catapult and horses. A spaceship playset could include a spaceship and a small refueling station. A "set" comprises all the pieces in a particular box, even if it includes multiple vehicles.

Studs—The "bumps" on top of LEGO bricks and plates. Real LEGO products have the word *LEGO* in tiny raised lettering on each stud.

Theme—A collection of several LEGO sets. When I was a kid, there were only three themes: Space, Castle, and Town. Today there are dozens, including Ninjago, Friends, City, and Galaxy Squad, as well as licensed themes like *Star Wars*, *The Hobbit*, *Teenage Mutant Ninja Turtles*, and Disney Princesses. Each of these themes has several sets at various price points, and understanding how the sets are grouped within a theme will make your students' design tasks easier.

LEGO on Paper: Designers at Work

Design a Minifigure

One of the great things about LEGO minifigures is their simple design. Although they've evolved slightly from the earliest smiley-faced little guys, they haven't changed much. That simplicity allows even young kids to work on designs representing characters from books, history, science, current events, etc. To be consistent with the simple design of the minifigures, I keep the related assignment, including the amount of required research, pretty simple. For example, if an action figure project takes students a class period or two, they should be able to bust out a few minifigures in half an hour.

I've had the greatest success when giving students multiple minifigure templates on one piece of paper. The template has four minifigures on it that they need to design to represent a group of characters. The assignment could be to design the four most important characters in a novel, or a historic archetype (explorer or leader) who changes over time, or four leaders of a particular movement. Sometimes, instead of a detailed biography, you want a quick and dirty version—actually, a quick and incredibly clean and wholesome version. Because they're children. The minifigure template is a great vehicle for this.

**Examples of
Student Work**

Design a Set

Designing LEGO sets is obviously a larger project than designing LEGO minifigures. Students design LEGO sets in multiple sizes, all pertaining to a specific theme. They're familiar with this because it's what they see on store shelves. For example, if there's a firefighting theme (and chances are very good there is one currently because

LEGO always has either police or fire in their lineup), there will be four sizes of sets:

1. **Small** = Fire chief's car with a fire extinguisher and single minifigure (around 100 pieces).
2. **Medium** = Fire helicopter with spinning rotors and two mini-figures (around 200 pieces).
3. **Large** = Fire truck putting out a building fire and three mini-figures (around 400 pieces).
4. **Huge-I'd-Love-as-an-Anniversary-Present** = Elaborate fire station with multiple fire engines, training equipment, and six minifigures (around 800 pieces).

Look at any given theme and you'll see these on multiple scales. A small *Star Wars* set, costing about ten dollars, will be available alongside a Millennium Falcon set costing ten times as much (okay, sometimes they're fourteen times as much). If I'm having students design LEGO sets on paper, I want them to be able to design at multiple scales, which requires a large historic event. The Great Depression could be the large coherent theme and students do research to develop four different sets to represent four different aspects of the era. For example:

1. **Small** = FDR in the Oval Office giving a fireside chat
2. **Medium** = Okies on the road to California
3. **Large** = Civilian Conservation Corps camp
4. **Huge** = Hoover Dam

Students design the sets on paper, including the related minifigures. You could have students design all four scales, or break students into groups and have each group create a different scale. You could assign one part of the class to focus on how big cities were affected by the Great Depression, while the other part concentrates on how it impacted rural Americans. Or part of the class might target the causes of the Depression while the other part focuses on New Deal programs trying to solve it. Students do research and become experts on smaller pieces of a very large historic event. Through these completed projects, students see a much bigger picture than they would have by reading a chapter from a book or even sitting through my PowerPoint presentation.

Examples of Student Work

"You don't have to be the bad guy. You are the most talented, most interesting, and most extraordinary person in the universe. And you are capable of amazing things. Because you are the Special. And so am I. And so is everyone. The prophecy is made up, but it's also true. It's about all of us. Right now, it's about you. And you...still...can change everything."

—Emmet, *The LEGO Movie*

HANDS-ON LEGO

Of course, actually building with LEGO is what kids want to do. It's what *I* want to do. While there's value in the LEGO design process noted above, a different set of skills, imagination, and understanding comes into play once students are *building*.

I would never use LEGO on the first day of school. Or the first week. Knowing myself and my middle school students, I need to have my classroom management and rules in place and my rapport with kids established, so they know exactly how much I'll flip out if LEGO bricks become projectiles or end up lodged in their noses!

When I use LEGO with my students, I usually just use the simple bricks, reserving the minifigures, wheels, wings, and windshields for specific projects. This encourages creativity and prevents some of the arguing over pieces and off-topic play. For example, if a group of four students is working on a project but there are only two minifigures, they'll be harassing each other for them. Of course, even without any special pieces, some students will still build giant swords and space-ships. They're kids! But some of that is prevented by eliminating the most playful pieces. (Wow, I sound like a tyrant.)

While LEGO is often a solitary activity, the interaction required for LEGO design group work is more valuable than some other group assignments. Having a limited set of resources (200 pieces for a group of four) forces discussion while students build. You can have students document their discussion, but what kid wants to be the scribe when she could be building with LEGO? I prefer to simply let them talk and have fun and then report on their discussion after they're finished playing with the toys. Don't kill the fun by making it all *assignmenty*.

I've used LEGO with my key history lessons. For example, when we study the causes of the American Revolution, students look at the events leading up to it, from the French and Indian War until the first shots fired at Lexington and Concord. After narrowing those events down to five, my students use LEGO to represent those crucial moments or significant events. In our Great Depression unit, students use LEGO to represent five different New Deal programs. In another unit, after studying monuments and memorials, they design a new monument for the National Mall in Washington, D.C. for an event or group of people without a major, national memorial in the nation's capital (World War I or the Iraq War, women, or Native Americans). Most students choose to design and build one for women or Native Americans, after getting over the outrage that there *isn't* one.

Building Prompts

Almost any writing prompt can be used as a building prompt. You can follow up the hands-on activity with a writing assignment to allow students to justify or give evidence for the choices they made during the design work. Some design prompts to consider are:

Examples of Student Work

General Classroom

- Classroom rules—Show a representation of one of the classroom rules.
- Classroom rules—Illustrate a rule you'd like to propose.
- Communication—Follow your partner's instructions to construct a (simple) LEGO building while blindfolded.
- Teambuilding—Collaborate on building one large LEGO structure.
- Classroom layout—Build a small diorama of how you think the room should be set up. (Later, you can vote on which layout students like best.)
- Design an ideal school—With your team, build different elements of what should be in a perfect school: classrooms, labs, cafeterias, gyms, common spaces, etc.

Science

- Biodiversity— Build your own animal or plant.
- Biomes—With your group, build the plants, animals, and landforms common to a specific biome.
- Animal and plant families—Build different members of the same families, focusing on the common characteristics which define the family.
- Molecule building—Using different colors to represent

different elements, combine bricks to form molecules.

- Cell structures—Build different cell structures that fit into one framework, but can be pulled out and examined separately.
- Dissection—Build the different organs and systems from an animal dissection.
- Inventions—Design an invention to solve a real-world problem.

Geography

- Landforms—Build landforms out of context.
- Physical map of your state—Build a desk-sized map of your state, focusing on the landforms, waterways, and geology of the region.
- Political map of your state—Add cities to the map, with towers representing different population sizes (each brick representing x number of residents).
- Map of your community—Highlight key features of your town or city.
- Current local events—Upgrade your community by solving specific problems.
- Dream vacation—Design and build your dream vacation location, complete with its landscape and activities.
- Cultural traits—Design costumes, foods, family structure, homes, etc. for a specific area.
- World landmarks—Use the UNESCO World Heritage sites to find landmarks to build in miniature.
- Demographics—Instead of using a bar graph, used LEGO towers to illustrate traits or statistics.
- Religious beliefs—Build a scene to represent key similarities, differences, and history of world religions.
- Economic and political systems—Create a scene to depict capitalism, communism, socialism, monarchy, theocracy, etc.

History (Scenes to Create)

- Events (causes and effects, outcomes, multiple perspectives, etc.)
- Timelines
- Ideas (abstract concepts, various "isms," etc.)
- Speeches (Lincoln's *Gettysburg Address*, FDR's *Four Freedoms*, MLK's *I Have a Dream*, JFK's *New Frontier*, Reagan's *Tear Down This Wall*)
- Preamble (the five duties of government)
- Bill of Rights (our different rights and freedoms)
- Biographies (show the five most important events in the life of a particular individual)
- Changing ideas of home and family
- Changing push and pull factors for immigration
- Causes of revolution
- Maps of empires
- Feudal systems
- Ancient cities
- Castles and forts
- Key Supreme Court cases
- Representation of wars
- Monuments and memorials to women, wars, heroes of peace
- Historic art and architecture

Language Arts

- Cover of a book
- Illustrations for a non-illustrated book
- Biographies of protagonists and antagonists
- Plot development
- Parts of speech
- Elements of an argumentative essay
- Settings in novels
- Character maps

Stop-Motion

LEGO is another toy that is ideal for stop-motion animation and, while time consuming, kids who want to make something different and high-quality enjoy the process. Designing and building the backgrounds, choosing which characters to use, and writing a script for the animation has to happen before actually doing the animating. These activities require research, synthesis, and summarization—all higher-level activities than you'd expect from "playing with toys." Searching "LEGO stop-motion" on YouTube yields about 1,320,000 results, so finding an example for your students is easy. Offer stop-motion alongside other projects, and you'll discover that kids are willing to invest a lot of time into something they're passionate about. Which is kind of the point.

More Ways to Incorporate LEGO in Your Classroom

So you've seen how I've used LEGO in my classroom, but if you want more ideas, The LEGO Group also has some official ways to get LEGO into the hands, minds, and hearts of students and teachers. The two best ones are FIRST LEGO League and LEGO Education.

First LEGO League

A few years ago my son's school started participating in FIRST LEGO League. Although I'm a card-carrying LEGO *maniac*, I didn't know much about it except that it included a robot competition, where kids built a LEGO-powered robot and completed certain tasks. I quickly learned a lot more. The robots run about $300, which stretches even my LEGO spending habits. But the school district used some technology funding and got dozens of its elementary schools—and hundreds of students—into the competition. My son stayed after school twice a week for months, learning how to program the robot, how to overcome the challenges the robot would encounter, and how to be a part of a team. Kids who are superfans of LEGO or technology aren't always the best "team players." My kid usually is because he's used to being part of a sports team. But he hadn't ever been part of a team that had to think, build, and problem solve together. FIRST LEGO League is all about this kind of team experience.

FIRST (**F**or **I**nspiration and **R**ecognition of **S**cience and **T**echnology) is an international, not-for-profit STEM engagement program for kids. FIRST and LEGO have worked together to build a program that challenges and enriches students from fourth through eighth grades. While the robots, and the tasks they complete, are the most visible part of the FIRST LEGO League competition, my favorite part is the three different presentations each team makes. The experience gives them the opportunity for public speaking, something most kids at this age don't often get to do. Teams explain how they incorporated into their project the FIRST LEGO League Core Values of Team Spirit, Integration, Discovery, Inclusion, and something LEGO calls "Coopertition." Coopertition acknowledges the event is a competition

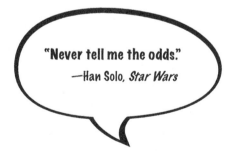

with one ultimate winner but emphasizes the fact that these challenges are meant to build up the other members of your team—and even the other teams. For example, twenty teams participated at a recent tournament. Teams were visiting with other teams and giving them small tokens of friendship—candy, stickers, or small dinosaurs (We're in Utah; dinosaurs happen now and then.). During the actual games, kids cheered for their team *and* for other teams—a pleasant change from the "kill 'em slugger!!" often synonymous with Little League-style sporting events.

Each year, FIRST LEGO League chooses a theme for the competition. One year, students designed robots to help senior citizens with different challenges. Last year, the theme focused on surviving natural disasters. Robots were designed to clear fallen limbs from power lines, rescue family pets, deliver food, fresh water, and medicine, and to clear debris from runways and streets. My son was inspired by the competition to think more about emergency preparedness and even made and posted to YouTube a stop-motion LEGO movie—*Tsunami Defense*—illustrating his own disaster plan.

FIRST LEGO League is a great venue for kids to learn, not just about robots and natural disasters but also about teamwork, leadership, and "Coopertition." Sure, it's a new word, but we could definitely use more of it!

LEGO Education

LEGO Education, another initiative LEGO actively supports, offers kits and programs with formal lesson plans and activities. Focusing on preschool through middle school classrooms and including curriculum for language arts, science, computer science, math, and engineering, these kits lead students through a building activity or problem-solving process from beginning to end. Similar to FIRST LEGO League, students in the upper grades shift toward programming and robotics, using the LEGO Mindstorms robotic systems. I like LEGO Education. A lot. Just be aware you're buying into a system which may make it harder to think outside the box. I want students to use the LEGO bricks, but I want to use them for dozens of different activities. You can certainly do this through the LEGO Education program, but I'd rather just have the bricks for my class.

First LEGO League   **LEGO Education**

THINGS TO THINK ABOUT

What favorite toy from your childhood could you share with your students?

How could you use other classic toys—Mr. Potato Head, Slinky, PEZ, Lincoln Logs, and army men—in your class?

What part(s) of your curriculum fit(s) best with toys?

How could asking your students to tell about *their* favorite toys build your classroom climate?

SECTION 2
GAMES

"Play is often talked about as if it were a relief from serious learning. But for children, play is serious learning. Play is really the work of childhood."

—Fred Rogers

"I am a Jedi, like my father before me."

—Luke Skywalker, *Star Wars*

"Logic is the beginning of wisdom, not the end."

—Spock, *Star Trek*

"Reality continues to ruin my life."

—Calvin, Calvin and Hobbes

GAMIFY YOUR
CLASSROOM

Adding even a simple game component can make a class more fun. Try it. Use a game element to let kids choose something related to a lesson: a die to change the course of a lesson or a spinner to choose an assignment. The element doesn't have to disrupt your entire class period; it simply adds a gamey randomness and makes it more fun.

Before I talk about how I use games in the classroom, I've got to plug the idea of *gamification* and the master of classroom gamification: Michael Matera. Michael is amazing! I've attended his presentations, become friends with him, seen his classroom via social media, and read his book, *Explore Like a Pirate*. He's able to transform—not just a class period or even a unit—but an entire school year into an extraordinary experience, simply by layering gaming principles and strategies onto his class's curriculum. (I'd give about anything to be a student in his class or have my sons in his class.) So if you're looking to overhaul your students' classroom experience, you need Michael's book. Not just because it has *pirate* in the title—but because it's extraordinary.

Following Michael's model, one sixth grade class in my area has a *gamified* medieval unit. Students don't stop talking about it—and don't forget it. Imagine if teachers gamified other units or the entire school year? Yes, it's a lot of work, but *Explore Like a Pirate* can guide you through it.

The games discussed in the following chapters can be done within a single class period—with set-up, game play, take-down, and content connections made within about an hour. Since part of the fun of games

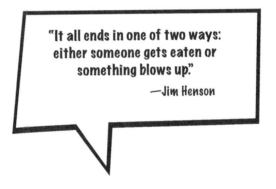

"It all ends in one of two ways: either someone gets eaten or something blows up."

—Jim Henson

is *playing* them, I don't want to use a bunch of class time explaining the rules of a complicated game. I like to keep things simple when it comes to my use of games in class.

Most of us have used *Jeopardy!* in our classrooms. *Jeopardy!* is great; I've used it as a review, too. But let's move beyond *Jeopardy!* and play games everyone in the class can participate in. And if you have a "Ken Jennings" (Just how many straight games of TV *Jeopardy!* did he win—like 150?), a "Hermione Granger," or a brainiac like Quinn Rollins in the room, you need to set up the game so they don't dominate. And, if they do dominate, you need to have a creative but legitimate way to limit their turns without seeming cruel.

A simple variant on *Jeopardy!* is "Trashketball." Students are divided into teams and as teams answer questions correctly, one of the team members gets to perform the physical feat of shooting a basketball into a trash can to earn points. What I love about this is the brainiacs may not be the best shooters, and the best shooters may not be the brainiacs. As a result, you get an entire team cheering for the student answering the question or shooting the basketball. Ironically, I don't allow "trash talk" among students playing Trashketball. Your classroom still needs to be a safe place for students. Well, safe except for the kid in fourth period determined to sacrifice his body to dunk the basketball into the trash can. So many rug burns!

A principle I include in any classroom game is that there will be losers. There will be winners, too, of course. But, in many classrooms, games end with, "You're all winners! Yay!" This undermines students' motivation to play games just as much as, "You're all losers! Boo!" Let kids lose. Don't destroy their lives or anything, but let them lose. They'll get over it by the next class period, and you'll give them another chance to win in a different game someday. But don't undermine the purpose of your game. Make the stakes of your game realistic by letting kids lose.

The Power of Play,
New York Times

Stuart Brown
TED Talk

HISTORY OF BOARD GAMES

Board games go back much further than most of us realize. Name an early civilization, and they had their own kind of board games. Ancient Egypt, China, Mesopotamia, the Indus Valley, Mesoamerica—they all had them. Some of those games have even remained popular into our own era, like Go, mancala, Parcheesi, chess, checkers, and tic-tac-toe. They're all classics that have a history. Like, before Atari®, even. Most board games, including classics such as Monopoly, Sorry!, Chutes and Ladders, Clue, and the Game of Life, possess similar elements: luck, strategy, tokens representing characters, a way to keep track of points, a game board to progress (and regress) through, and a clear winner. While the popularity of video games might have us thinking that the heyday of board games is behind us, recent games like Settlers of Catan and Ticket to Ride have proven there's still a market for them. We still love our board games.

9

BOARD GAMES

The mention of board games brings up (deceptive) images of quiet evenings spent with family members—munching on popcorn, and politely passing the dice to the next player. Reality, however, is often much different and much more exciting. In fact, some of my favorite memories with friends and family were made while playing games—raucous, competitive, hilarious games. Over card games, I've bonded with friends and strengthened family ties. And I'll never forget the time my sweet grandmother played a certain swear word in Scrabble when she could have used those same letters to spell *T-H-I-S* or *H-I-T-S* or even *S-I-T-H*. Oh, Grandma! Or when my wife threw an Othello board across the room after losing to her sister, or when my friend nearly killed me after drawing forty-two cards in a game of UNO. The point is: board games aren't as sedate as you might think. And that's what makes them fun!

In the classroom, games can provide opportunities for students to recall information or processes on the fly instead of regurgitating a lecture or filling in a bubble on a worksheet. The activity is still an assessment—and it's fun! Plus, students are pushed to move past recall, into extended and strategic thinking. Students become aware of the tactics they're using and how to use them strategically to get ahead in the game. Students are then using metacognition and cross into true critical thinking. And the great thing is they're doing the *metacogniting* (like the new word I just made up?) and probably don't realize it unless you ask them to reason out why they're doing what they're doing. But I wouldn't do that often—just enough times to grease the wheels. Help them recognize they play the way they do for a reason.

Most games require social interaction which can really help involve students who are shy or reserved. I tend to be shy in certain settings, and it's hard for me to have conversations with people I've never met or people I'm forced into a group with. Playing a game with others gives me something to focus on beside my discomfort. As I'm playing, paying attention to the rules and trying to win, I get to know the other players, but in a more comfortable setting. If playing games helps me this way, it may also help students who have a lot to offer but tend to be more introverted.

"Junior" versions are available of many of the most popular games, including Scrabble, Monopoly, Settlers of Catan, Risk, and Boggle. While these are intended for younger children, they have streamlined play and pieces, making them preferable for classroom use. Rather than a regular game of Monopoly (which can take hours) or Scrabble (which is too broad for most curricula), the junior versions are easier and use the same strategies, which is what you really want.

Likewise, most card games are relatively quick to play, and our students have played many of them. Games like UNO, Rook, Mille Bornes, or Skip-Bo are easy to adapt into a classroom game. Other games like Dominion and Guillotine are more elaborate and have less repetitive gameplay, but are worth checking out.

Newer to those of us of a "certain age" are the European-styled board games popularized over the last fifteen or twenty years: Settlers of Catan, Carcassonne, and Ticket to Ride. Typically, these have a more extended strategy than the board games I grew up with, and they have some excellent classroom applications. Each requires players to accumulate resources, map out targets in advance, and predict what other players will do with their own resources. The historic variations of these particular three games are an added bonus for history teachers, like me. For example, Ticket to Ride: The Heart of Africa adds "Terrain Cards," which help navigate special obstacles in the continent's geography. New World: A Carcassonne Game begins on the East Coast of North America, with players gathering settlers and collecting resources so they can move into the continent. While these games seem to be geared toward history, geography, and social studies, I've also seen them used as jumping-off points for discussions about resource management, as writing prompts, and as setups for math problems with

> "Sometimes I lie awake at night and I ask, 'Is life a multiple choice test or is it a true-or-false test?' ...then a voice comes to me out of the dark and says, 'We hate to tell you this, but life is a thousand-word essay.'"
> —Charles Schulz

real-world applications. Other high-level games include Pandemic, which requires communication and cooperation between players who are trying to stop four diseases from destroying the world. Another is The Resistance, a variation on the "mafia" game I used to play as a kid, where players try to resist a corrupt government, while avoiding spies and completing missions.

CREATING YOUR OWN BOARD GAMES

There have been times I've wanted a very specific board game—on Utah's mining history, for example. It turns out there's not a store-bought game available on that particular topic. Crazy, I know. So I made my own. I discovered the easiest way to do this is to use an existing template.

Before selecting a template, think about the experience you want students to have. Do you want a game where "everybody wins"? Can you have a game with only one winner but where all the students learn your objective? One lesson my mining game makes clear is that, historically, mining wasn't an enterprise where everyone would strike it

My Board Game

rich. Mining required a lot of hard work. Success depended on luck, and it was subject to outside factors, like transportation, imports, and exports. My game needed to reflect all those factors.

I drew my game board with a series of squares, using Candy Land as my inspiration. One difference (aside from not including the Chocolate Swamp or Peppermint Forest) was to place the *start* square exactly in the middle. At the upper (winning) end of the board was the Mine Owner's Mansion. At the bottom of the board, The Pit. I placed a stack of about fifty cards with factors that would make mines more profitable (war production increases demand for metals), less profitable (import tariffs drop), or have an uncertain effect (workers unionize). During play, students draw a card and move forward or backward the number of spaces allowed. If the card notes a factor with an uncertain effect, students only move forward if they can explain how that factor could either be good or bad for mining. In the course of the game, players moved forward and backward, getting close to the mansion, then getting pulled back. It very quickly becomes evident that mining was a potentially volatile industry, with some progress and a lot of setbacks. At the end of the game, we debrief, discussing the factors which moved them forward and backward in the game, and identify and explain things they had questions about. Overall, students acquired a deeper understanding than they would have from my lecture or their reading because it had a real-world consequence for them—even if only for a single class period.

This same gameplay could be used with any topic involving forward and backward movement: immigration, civil rights, environmental protection, economic growth, and international diplomacy. This is also a great model to use when you want to demonstrate how shifting factors play into an uncertain status quo. Sometimes you want students to see a long-term trend in a particular direction. For example, the overall trend of civil rights in the United States has been toward

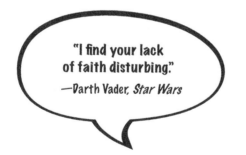

"I find your lack of faith disturbing."
—Darth Vader, *Star Wars*

more freedoms for more people. In this case, stack the deck with more forward-moving cards, but still include the setbacks. Do the opposite when you want students to feel the need for change. For instance, if I want students to become aware of problems regarding endangered species extinction, I'd make the cards stacked against those animals. Yes, even against cute little pandas.

Include candy or other tangible awards in a game—as long as your students' parents won't string you up for it. I have another mining game

(I *do* teach more than just mining) using Smarties candy. Students get a roll of Smarties as their land claim, and each of the six colors of candy represents a different mineral. Yellow is gold, the others are coal, iron, copper, lead, and zinc. Students tally up how many of each mineral they have, and if they have more than three pieces of "gold," they strike it rich. We then talk about what they would do with their money: spend it (open the roll, eat the candy now) or invest it in additional claims (get additional rolls of Smarties). We play three rounds, and by the end of the third round, the richest students have up to six or seven rolls of Smarties, while most of the class are left with just their original roll. This prompts a discussion about fairness, inequality, and how the rich in society might keep getting richer, while others stay at about the same level. If they're lucky. The same gameplay could be used for other inequalities such as who's born on a particular continent, genetic characteristics, water distribution, etc. Life, sadly, is not fair.

Students Create
Their Own Board Games

Creating games for my students requires me to think about every possible outcome, every strategy they might use, every question they might have, and every piece of content I want to get into the game. It's a lot more thinking and designing than any single player might encounter for the game. Having students design their own board games and then play those games with other kids is an excellent way to assess their learning as it requires they think about and use the material in a unique way. I typically do this activity a few units after my classes have played my board games, so they have an idea of my expectations and how they're able to meet them.

Each student starts with the same template, something simple, like Candy Land, Chutes and Ladders, or Monopoly. They can then modify it, making it more complex if they like. I give them a checklist or range of content they're expected to incorporate into the game in a way that makes sense to the student and the players. Gameplay can follow the template, or they can make it more complicated. Because most kids spend a lot more time playing games every day than I do, they come up with additions, layers, and levels to make the game more complex than the simple template I give them. I stipulate that the game must be winnable by at least one player, but other than that, students have free rein. So many of our students dream of being video game designers. Letting them design a game on paper gives them a simple view of the process and takes them a step toward that dream job. And if you've got someone at your school with the background to help students move their game design into the digital realm, all the better.

CONTENT CRUSHES

In *Teach Like a PIRATE*, Dave Burgess writes about different kinds of passion we should use in the classroom: passion for pedagogical practice, personal passions (which this book is about), and passion for the content you teach. When my class comes to a unit I absolutely love, I tell them it is my history *crush*. World War I and the Great Depression are my crushes. Really? I know, their appeal was lost on me for a while, also. I mean, World War II is easy to love—it's horrific, it's the worst of humanity, and the best of humanity. Plus it's the greatest victory—especially since we view ourselves as the heroes. And because of thousands of books, probably hundreds of movies, and video games, the kids come in knowing about World War II and already love it. I confess to students I used to skim over World War I and the Great Depression because I didn't know much about them. But I also tell them I learned more, went to workshops, read some fiction, found primary sources written by people who lived through them—and "fell in love."

I use my own story of falling in love with my history crushes to inspire them to get excited about what they are going to learn. Even if they don't end up sharing my love for the topic, they know I am head over heels for it. It isn't just another boring chapter; this is *this thing Rollins loves*!

Your passion might be DNA, isosceles triangles (the coolest of triangles), or diagramming sentences (Can you *really* have a crush on such a thing?). Use that science crush, geometry crush, or language arts crush to bring your subject to life in a brand new way for your students. What are the pieces of your content which made you want to teach that subject? When you reach them in your curriculum, go bonkers!

HISTORY OF MINECRAFT

Minecraft may be the most recent game of those featured in this book, but it's moved past the realm of "game" and become a full-on phenomenon. It has its own awe-inspiring creation myth, how the programmer known as "Notch" (Markus Persson) quit his job in Stockholm to work on building the game that would become Minecraft. That was in 2009. During the following two years, he tested and released smaller beta versions, until the game was getting ready for primetime. By late 2011, Minecraft became available for purchase on the wider market. Almost immediately, it began crashing servers because the users were growing faster than the system could handle them. Minecraft has maintained that level of popularity for the past five years, and isn't showing any sign of slowing down. The game's developers keep things fresh for established users by regularly releasing updates (You can farm salmon now!), yet maintain its core simplicity, so newbies aren't at a disadvantage. Sign up Monday morning, and you're having fun by the afternoon.

MINECRAFT

I learned how to play Minecraft watching over my sons' shoulders. They started with small cabin-style houses, upgraded to large farms, and eventually built elaborate mansions. A constant through the entire learning process has been what they can do with a block of TNT. Is there a kid out there who doesn't like to blow things up? I can't think of any. In early days, that meant setting traps with a land mine-style pressure plate so zombies blow up. As they learned how to use things like "redstone" (which conducts the Minecraft version of electricity), and levers, switches, and buttons, now they can blow things up from further away, unleashing power that would make the Death Star pale in comparison. And while I don't necessarily want them doing that in my backyard, I love that they're learning the elements of coding and other skills that can help them in programming and engineering. I've experienced Minecraft more as a dad than as a teacher, watching my sons discover and learn to use the game—placing and breaking blocks in a 3D world—and become obsessed with it.

The Minecraft learning arc generally progresses like this:

- Build in your own world.
- Interact with other players in other worlds.
- Play games other players have created.
- Build more complicated structures and machines based on what you've observed in other worlds.
- Build games you can play with a limited number of players in your own world.
- Build games anyone can play.

FROM THE PLAY ROOM TO THE CLASSROOM

As I've watched my sons progress through these stages in the world of Minecraft, I've discovered that each one has classroom application. Isolated in their own worlds, your students can begin building in solitude—a good way to give your students "training wheels" while they're learning. However, half of our students will likely know more about Minecraft than we, the clueless adults in their lives, will ever

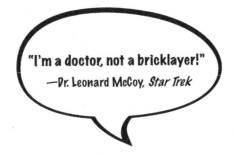

"I'm a doctor, not a bricklayer!"
—Dr. Leonard McCoy, *Star Trek*

know. That's why an even better approach to Minecraft is to have students work collaboratively (or competitively). If you have a classroom "world" set up on a server, only your students will have access it. No trolls, no weirdos. Just your kids. To be fair, some of them probably *are* trolls and weirdos, but you'll know who they are.

If you allow students to work in "Creative Mode" in your class world, they'll have unlimited resources with which to build. In "Survival Mode," they need to "mine" and find resources, but if they learn initially in Creative Mode, they can build anything. I've heard Minecraft compared to having an infinite box of LEGO and an infinite space to build in. Pretty accurate comparison, I'd say. As such, the classroom applications are almost as infinite. Here are some examples of building projects you could assign to students:

- Ancient civilizations: Babylonian/Egyptian/Greek/Roman/ Chinese
- World War I trenches and supply lines
- A model of your community
- New civic buildings for your community
- Monument or memorial to a great person or event
- Food production and distribution
- Space station or lunar colonies
- Transit system
- Historic or modern urban planning
- Medieval castles and villages
- Layout of a fictional book's setting
- Rube Goldberg machines

Kids love Minecraft. They spend hours building and just as many hours watching videos on YouTube of how other kids have solved problems and built elaborate structures. Chances are very good some of your students have made walk-through videos of their own projects. If students are into Minecraft, they're very devoted to it, and just as devoted to learning how to do it all better.

As students learn to play Minecraft, they acquire sets of skills to advance their abilities in the game. These skills—coding rules, typing, simple math, machines, the process of turning raw materials into finished goods, collaboration and teamwork, chemical reactions, compounds, extended thinking and planning, and even simple economics—are skills students will utilize far beyond Minecraft play.

Several Minecraft clones are now available, and some of them are pretty good. Starmade, for example, is essentially Minecraft in space, so if you had an elective class about space exploration, this would be a fun approach. Blockheads is available as a mobile app, and while players don't have as many options as they do in Minecraft, it's easier to play and connect to other players. ROBLOX may be the most challenging of these types of games because it focuses on *building* the games as well as playing them. Students spend more time coding and programming in ROBLOX, making it ideal for STEM classes.

MinecraftEdu

Similar to LEGO Education, MinecraftEdu is a formal way to bring Minecraft into your classroom. MinecraftEdu assists teachers in setting up classroom servers and provides bulk discounts on licenses. This makes Minecraft a realistic and affordable option for many schools. They offer prepackaged lesson plans and teacher tutorials. While we may never catch up with our students, the tutorials give us a fighting chance and enable us to help our non-Minecrafty kids learn how to play.

MinecraftEdu

Teaching in the age of Minecraft, *The Atlantic*

Getting started with MinecraftEDU, *Educade*

Top 10 Minecraft Creations selected by Watchmojo.com, YouTube video

MEETING STUDENTS WHERE THEY ARE

Let's face it—we're old. We're teachers, and in the eyes of our students, we're ancient. Even if you're a twenty-three-year-old, first-year teacher—just five years older than your seniors—you may as well be their grandmother. So my pop culture reference to *Three's Company* isn't going to make any sense to my students. And using the word "Mayberry" to refer to a small town? They won't get it. We need to learn more about current pop culture so we can use it with our students. Through my students, I discovered *Phineas and Ferb*, which led to using a platypus secret agent in a classroom activity. I learned about Justin Bieber the same way and also learned exactly how much I could make fun of him before I made the boys laugh and the girls cry. New apps, new games, and new books—I learn about them all through my students. In fact, I read *The Hunger Games* books before they became movies because every single kid in my classes was reading them. Keeping their current pop culture in mind, I can make more current references than my joke about Gopher on *The Love Boat*—which was an incredibly funny joke! Using references to things your kids already like and understand will help you make your lessons more relevant to them, and your students will get your point a whole lot faster.

HISTORY OF TRADING CARDS

The history of trading cards is rooted in sports cards—primarily baseball cards. Released in 1887, the first series of baseball cards was part of a larger set of sports cards, including boxing, golf, and horse racing. Sports cards continued to be produced off and on until 1902, when baseball cards erupted as a collectible item. Until the 1930s, companies experimented with the format, changing the sizes of the cards and what product they would come in. Sometimes cards came in Cracker Jack boxes, sometimes with bubble gum or tobacco. During the 1930s, manufacturers decided on a consistent size and on bubble gum as the product of choice. The 1970s brought an explosion of television series and movie trading cards. Then, in 2000, trading cards got another boost with the *Pokémon* phenomenon, Magic: The Gathering, and other games. The hook with trading cards is the more you collect, the more power you have, and the more games you win. So, of course, you want to collect them all.

TRADING CARDS

While I'm sure a collector somewhere is trying to find his last *Three's Company* or *Laverne & Shirley* trading card, my cards of choice were *Star Wars* (shocker, I know!). In fact, I've only ever collected two series of trading cards: movie cards from *The Empire Strikes Back* and *Transformers* trading cards. The movie cards mostly told the story of the movie for those of us unfortunate enough to live before Blu-Ray, Netflix, DVDs, and even VHS! But they also had some fascinating biography cards for the main characters. The Transformer cards, for the most part, were biography cards for the fifty or so main Autobots and Decepticons but had some story cards as well.

TRADING CARDS IN THE CLASSROOM

Lots of great templates are available for making history trading cards. Most of them boil down to a microbiography—summarizing someone's life in the space the size of a single playing card. (I generally use a 4" x 6" template, but you get the idea.) The templates are based on baseball cards, *Pokémon* cards, or Magic: The Gathering cards, and have space for a picture, a short biographical sketch, and a few stats or rankings. My personal template combines several of those elements, including one I borrowed from LEGO Ninjago trading cards. Those cards come with the Ninjago toys, and kids read them to learn how to play (and win) the Ninjago game. By looking at the cards, kids can quickly summarize a character and evaluate what kinds of situations that character could be put in. My template—as well as the strategies I suggest for how to *use* trading cards—uses this same approach.

**Examples of
Student Work**

Biographies are the most straightforward use of trading cards; after all, the baseball cards many of us grew up with were about people. They're great to use in a unit with a broad theme, like my Westward Expansion unit, during which I highlight about sixty individuals involved in some aspect of this period of history. Students self-select eight of those individuals, read single-page biographies about them, and then distill the most important parts of each person's biography onto a single card.

Trading cards are also great to use with storylines or anything involving a series of events. For a novel, students could design one card per chapter to keep track of what's happening in the story. For a sequence of historic events, one card could be made per year or one per milestone event. Scientific processes, like evolution or cell division, could be represented by one card per defined stage.

Trading cards can also span themes. Key battles from wars, inventions that changed the course of history, geographical features, or countries of the world can be taught with this tool. Science, scientists, branches of science you're teaching, the tools of science, the scientific method, and how it developed can also be tracked with trading cards. Or use them in a music class to highlight periods of classical music, composers, instruments, or musical notations. Trading cards are also great to use in math classes to outline equations, formulas, and their real-world applications. Essentially, any content area with multiple elements can be transformed into the trading card format.

Online Trading Card Generators

WAYS TO USE TRADING CARDS IN CLASS

Many teachers make flashcards to help students remember things. Students use them to cram for a test, but after the test, those flashcards hit the recycle bin. My goal for trading cards is more long term. Many card games could be altered slightly to make a classroom game to deepen a student's understanding of the importance of characters, concepts, or processes. If your students made cards to last for multiple units, you'd be able to show them the lasting value of what they're learning throughout the school year and help them remember in April that—*oh, yeah!*—we did learn something last October.

Using a high school language arts class as an example, this model could be used with four separate units:

Unit One
Of Mice and Men

Unit Two
The Scarlet Letter

Unit Three
The Great Gatsby

Unit Four
The Grapes of Wrath
(I know—another Steinbeck—but I don't care. I love him.)

For each novel, students would make, say, ten trading cards highlighting protagonists, antagonists, settings, themes, catalysts for the characters or plot, and author biographies. After Unit Two, students would be able to compare and contrast characters and other points of the novels. Who's the better character? How did each approach obstacles? If we swapped Hester Prynne of *The Scarlet Letter* with Curley's wife from *Of Mice and Men*, how would it change both stories? Is the change only because the novels are set in different time periods? Or is the change more dramatic because of their personalities? And how does the fact that we know exponentially more about Hester than we do about Curley's wife affect our opinion of the two women?

The traditional approach is to assign an essay at this point. However, I believe students who compare these two characters, a second set of characters, and then a theme will benefit more from a single class period than from busting out a five-paragraph essay.

After Unit Three, add in characters from *The Great Gatsby*, and characters from *The Grapes of Wrath* after Unit Four. By this point, students are comparing four different novels. You know why you've

"I don't want to survive.
I want to live."
—Captain B. McCrea, *WALL-E*

selected these four books for students to study, but the benefits of your initial purpose will likely expand as students use these trading cards to enhance their own knowledge and literary experience. Since I'm a fan of reading and of student writing, it is at this point that I would assign an essay. The background they'll have to pull from after comparing four books, instead of just two, will be much deeper and more complex.

Students will retain much more from your course using trading cards than they will by doing a memory dump after Unit One, which is what 84 percent of students do. (Okay, I have no data to back that up—it's a percentage I made up. But I bet it's pretty close to accurate. Maybe.)

So, your students have read four novels and have made forty trading cards. Now the games begin! You could use the **Magic: The Gathering** format and have kids play their characters against each other and decide which would win each confrontation. Characters can be leveled up or down with events from their books. For example, Arthur Dimmesdale gets hit by the Dust Bowl! Boom!

You could use the **Apples to Apples** format where kids use cards from their novel to answer questions you ask. For example, you provide cards with personality traits (perseverance, sliminess) or scenarios ("Who's most likely to win on *Survivor*?" Or "Who would give you the coat off his/her back?" Or "Who would steal my car?"), and students select the "character" card they believe best fits your question. You could also ask questions to which students can play their "setting" cards, such as, "Which fictional setting would you most like to live in?" or "Which setting most closely resembles your own community?" In response to a question about which protagonist they would choose for president, each student throws down a card they think best answers that question. For each question, they need to defend their choice against the choices made by other students.

Following the **Guillotine** format, each character card is assigned a point value and lined up in a row, moving inexorably toward "execution" (the point where a student picks up the card and collects the points for that card). Events changing the order of the line can be noted on separate "action" cards or may simply be called out by the teacher. Students strategize to use the events to maximize their potential to "execute" as many high-point characters as possible.

Students can also play the **Card on the Forehead** game, where one student, without looking at it first, places the back of a character card on his forehead. The other student describes the character from the card without using the title, author of the book, or the names of other characters in the book.

Memory is another great card game. Cards from all the novels are placed face-down on a table. Students turn cards over two at a time, trying to make a pair. Students can make any kind of match as long as they can explain the connection between the cards and provide evidence from the novels.

Simple card matching games can be used with almost any curriculum. For example, in a science class, students can make cards related to the forces shaping the earth's surface. You project an image on the screen of a particular element of the earth's geography, and they match the picture to the force creating it.

While there are likely countless ways to play games with trading cards, the overall takeaway is this: if students make the trading cards, they should at least collect them. Just doing that is cool. I've collected trading cards—it's fun! And it's better to have them do *something* with those cards, besides put a rubber band around them and tuck them in a folder. But playing games with them is even better! As students play—even on their own—they reinforce their understanding of characters and concepts. Better yet, if they're playing with other students, they see how those kids made trading cards about the same content, but possibly used different characters, or how their own cards are similar or different from the cards of others. All of this works to create a deeper and more rewarding experience for your students—and *you*. What pieces of your class content could be used to create trading cards?

WEIRD HOLIDAYS

Once a week, find a holiday to celebrate. You don't need to have a party; just hang a sign on the board or refer to it in class. October 3 is National Virus Day. May 16 is Sea Monkey Day. January 18 is Winnie the Pooh Day. Some of these have reasoning behind them (January 18 was the birth date of Pooh's creator, A. A. Milne), but others are as random as they seem. If you have a personal connection to one of those weird holidays, exploit it. If it happens to tie into your curriculum, awesome! Just have fun with it. Every year, I celebrate Talk like a Pirate Day (September 19) and St. Patrick's Day (March 17), both of which allow me to talk with a ludicrous accent (actually, my Pirate and Irish accents kind of slur into each other by the end of the day). On St. Patrick's Day, I call students by their last names as much as possible, but add a "Mc" or "O'" to the beginning of them. My favorites are names which aren't Irish. At all. "That's a great answer, Miss O'Martinez!" "What do you think, Mr. McKlopferschmidt?" It doesn't derail the class, but we all have fun with it.

Section 3

Superheroes, Graphic Novels, and Comic Strips

"The most sophisticated people I know—inside they are all children."
—Jim Henson

"Some people can read *War and Peace* and come away thinking it's a simple adventure story. Others can read the ingredients on a chewing gum wrapper and unlock the secrets of the universe."
—Lex Luthor, *Superman: The Movie*

"Comics have been decried as fostering illiteracy. It's tosh. It's snobbery and it's foolishness. There are no bad authors for children that children like and want to read and seek out because every child is different. They can find the stories they need to, and they bring themselves to stories."
—Neil Gaiman

"Beep-beep, bwoop-brt."
—R2-D2, *Star Wars*

RECENT(-ISH) HISTORY
OF SUPERHEROES

The late 1970s and early 1980s were a great time to love superheroes. The classic Adam West *Batman* series was in reruns, *Challenge of the Superfriends* and *Spider-Man and His Amazing Friends* were there on Saturday mornings, and *He-Man*, *Thundercats*, and *Voltron* were on during the day. The superheroes were mostly on the small screen, but Christopher Reeve's *Superman* was out there, too, and our imaginations soared alongside The Man of Steel.

Looking back, that all seems quaint compared to what's happening right now. Avengers, X-Men, Justice League, they're all on the big screen and have become more a part of pop culture and the everyday conversation in homes and classrooms around the world. Kids know the origin stories, the superpowers, and the enemies of these characters more than ever before. It's a source of knowledge ripe for the taking.

SUPERHEROES

I love superheroes. A lot. When I was a kid, I didn't miss watching *SuperFriends.* I watched Lynda Carter's *Wonder Woman* and Adam West's *Batman* (in reruns, but still). These characters fueled my imagination. And it wasn't just me. On the playground, my friends and I would pretend to be the Wonder Twins and try to reach hands so we could "activate" our powers and turn into an animal and something made of ice, water, or steam, I guess. I made my own Batman utility belt, complete with (don't try this at home, kids) a Batarang and grappling hook. And I know that it's hip these days to hate on Aquaman, but he was the Super Friend I liked best. His command of the seas intrigued me as much as Superman's command of the skies. These were more than just comic book characters for me.

My love of these heroes continued on into adulthood. I actually started reading the books these characters came from. I love the stories. They're layered, complex characters, written by authors and artists who love them as much as I do. I still use comic book references in daily conversation—my parents' house is the Batcave, and if something is super-fast, it's like the Flash. I joke sometimes that I wouldn't marry my wife until she could name the seven members of the Justice League. What makes it funny (or sad) is that it was a trick question. There weren't seven members of the Justice League; there were *twelve*. Plus secret identities for five of them. (I wanted her to know exactly what she was signing up for.) Yes, I know—and love—superheroes.

WAYS TO USE EXISTING SUPERHEROES IN THE CLASSROOM

I've been using superheroes in the classroom since my first year of teaching. And it's only gotten easier and more relevant over time. With comic book characters being as prominent as they are in pop culture these days, references to them provide an instant connection with many of my students. A decade ago, only a handful of your students would have known who the Avengers were. Now, it would be hard to find a kid who couldn't name them and their superpowers. That familiarity gives teachers families of characters we can use to make allegories, to tell stories, and to make connections. Essentially, when we use superheroes as examples, we're speaking the same language as our students. And even if they're super-mature, uh, eighth graders, they know these characters. Between their excitement that you're using things they already understand in class and their nostalgia for their own (super-distant) childhood, they'll love it. Here are a few ways to tie superheroes into your lessons.

- Myths—Explore how classical gods have allegories that are found in prominent heroes of Marvel and DC Comics.
- Modern myths—If the Avengers, Justice League, et al. are a modern myth, what could they represent?
- Trace Joseph Campbell's *The Hero's Journey* through various superheroes' stories.

- How could superheroes be used to reinforce classroom/school goals and norms?
- Look at how superheroes can represent core principles for society.
- Trace how the "heroism" of superheroes has changed over time, for example, from Captain America to Wolverine to Punisher to Deadpool.
- Analyze how real-world events, such as World War II, Vietnam, or 9/11 are reflected (or ignored) in comic books.
- Contrast the roles of male and female superheroes.
- Consider the archetype of the sidekick—can young people be their own heroes without an adult leading them?
- Most superheroes have an "archenemy"—Superman's Lex Luthor and Batman's Joker—do these characters have their own Hero's Journey?

HAVE STUDENTS DESIGN AND USE THEIR OWN SUPERHEROES

Some heroes clearly represent certain ideas. Captain America is probably the best example; you can't miss the fervent patriotism at the core of his character. Recent movies have played with this image—suggesting Captain America is too corny or too dated for the twenty-first century. But for the purposes of our classrooms, he's an excellent example. If Captain America exemplifies the patriotism of the 1940s, use him as a template to design your own superheroes representing different abstract concepts. For example, in a social studies class, you could have students redesign Captain America to be a superhero from another country: Captain Panama, Captain Australia, Captain Kenya, and Captain Tibet would each have some distinct possibilities. How would the students reflect the culture, geography, or the politics of the new hero's homeland? Could a female Captain be a better representation of that culture? How about redesigning the hero to be Captain Original America and represent a particular tribe or culture of Native Americans?

If you want to stick to Captain Regular America, students could also redesign him to represent a different time period. For example, Captain America: 1812 would likely have a different costume, mission, and set of superpowers than the Steve Rogers we know. Captain America: 2016 would possibly depart even further from our traditional Cap.

Students could create original superheroes to depict different time periods. A Justice League comprised of heroes representing the Industrial Revolution might include elements of steam power, mechanization, urbanization, and immigration in their ranks. The X-Men of the Han Dynasty might include Confucius, a dragon, and jade.

**Examples of
Student Work**

Students could make superheroes from the "powers" delineated in the Constitution: the legislative, judicial, and executive branches. Each is its own superhero (or villain if you want to go there) team. Each person (not power) is a superhero, with a unique ability. So the Executive Team would include a Veto Girl; the Judicial Team would have Judicial Review Lad. I know that as a kid, that would have reinforced my understanding of what those branches could actually do, and be more interesting than that dumb triangular chart that I've probably filled out 400 times in my life.

Superheroes can be incorporated into virtually any subject. In language arts, the heroes could be punctuation. They could be prefixes and suffixes, they could be spelling conventions. In a health class, you could flip the strategy around and have students create a "Legion of Doom" team of supervillains featuring bad habits or substances that would endanger their health. A physics unit could include superheroes representing mass, inertia, velocity, kinetic, and potential energy. In each case, the superheroes are building blocks for a greater understanding. Students connecting those building blocks will make reaching the next level of understanding easier.

The superhero strategy can be used beyond classroom curriculum as well. For example, a student who designs a superhero representing a classroom rule—ideally one she had some input in creating—will potentially implement and follow the rule better than others. And take a look at school mascots. Many of them have nothing to do with the environment, culture, or history of the location of their schools. They're chosen seemingly at random or maybe because of alliteration (Go Bennion Bobcats!). Give students the opportunity to design a mascot using a superhero template, instructing them to be able to defend why they chose a particular animal, historic figure, or geographic feature. In my community, one of the few, genuinely historic mascots is the Jordan Beetdigger. Because the people farmed sugar beets. There's even an enormous bronze statue of a beet in their hallway. Personally, I'd rather have this type of mascot, rather than one with no connection to the community.

The Superhero as Society's Mirror, from WWII to Iraq, *New York Times*

MOVIE CLIPS YOU LOVE

This is where I rave about how good *Forrest Gump* is for teaching history classes. Except I won't—because I've never actually seen it. An admission that makes people drop their jaws and want to strap me in a chair *Clockwork Orange*-style, hold my eyes open with hooks, and make me watch the entire movie.

If you teach history, you already know about *Forrest Gump*. If you teach music, you know how to use pieces of *Mr. Holland's Opus* in your class. Civics teachers know *Twelve Angry Men*. You know the movies related to your curriculum. That's great. But it isn't the only way to use movies to connect with kids.

I'm going to suggest you find clips of movies you love *just because* you love them. Taking three minutes to show a clip from *Toy Story 2, Jaws, Gone With the Wind*, or *The Muppet Movie;* just because it makes you happy doesn't hurt anything. Making you, the teacher, happy does something positive for your class that day—it sets the mood and establishes the climate you want. Be creative. Show a YouTube clip of some guy doing incredible parkour or maybe a really funny clip from Jimmy Fallon. So what if the clip has absolutely nothing to do with the Oregon Trail? It made me laugh, and laughing helps us talk about why dysentery killed every single person in the Oregon Trail game.

HISTORY OF COMIC BOOKS

In the late 1920s and early 1930s, publishers experimented with small pamphlets and magazines that reprinted comic strips from the week's newspapers. Some were sold, others were given away, but they really didn't find any sort of mass audience. That changed in 1938, when DC Comics published Jerry Siegel's and Joe Shuster's "Superman" as the cover story for *Action Comics* #1. From that issue through the end of World War II, comic lovers saw an explosion of colorful superhero stories. Superman was joined by Batman, Robin, Wonder Woman, Captain Marvel, the Human Torch, Captain America, and the Flash. Comic books were cheap to produce and ship, so thousands of soldiers overseas ended up with copies to help them pass the time. Despite a rocky period during the 1950s, when comic books were accused of corrupting the youth of America in every way imaginable, comic books have remained a part of pop culture ever since. Some people like to try to class up comic books by calling them "sequential art" or "visual storytelling," but for me, they're comic books. Don't be ashamed of them.

Comic Books and Graphic Novels

While my first exposure to superheroes was through television, I started reading comic books pretty early. The first comic book I ever bought with my own money was *Star Wars #11*. It had Luke Skywalker on a rocket boat, fighting a sea monster—and losing. C-3PO and R2-D2 were being knocked overboard. It was completely unlike anything I had seen Luke do in the first *Star Wars* movie, and I bought it. And devoured it. The first superhero comic book I ever read was a Teen Titans book that was handed out to schools. Basically an anti-drug public service announcement that I didn't quite understand as a kid, but I loved seeing those heroes in action. These weren't my *SuperFriends* from TV, but they were similar. I learned new words, like "cyborg" and "empath," and got to know a new family of characters. My love for superheroes—and reading about them—got me hooked on comic books and graphic novels.

As I grew older, I realized that other genres of comic books were available. Some were still fiction, but they told stories without capes and masks. Others were non-fiction and deftly told stories using words and pictures as an integrated art form. It's funny that we endorse combining pictures with words as a good way to tell stories to young children, but as they get older, we want children to abandon their picture books. As with other strategies I recommend in this book, I'd argue the things we valued as children still have value for us as adults—and at every age in between.

Finding a personal passion for comic books and graphic novels will help you teach your students. As the parent of a son who *can* read, but *hates* reading, finding out he loved graphic novels was an epiphany. I'd even bought books I thought he'd like, but for some reason I didn't think he'd like graphic novels. Then, I brought home some copies of *Nathan Hale's Hazardous Tales*, a graphic novel series which retells stories from American history. In an unusually serendipitous turn, they're

"Words and pictures are yin and yang. Married, they produce a progeny more interesting than either parent."
—Dr. Seuss

written and illustrated by a guy named (yes, you guessed it) Nathan Hale. And the Revolutionary War spy, Nathan Hale, is the narrator. It's all very meta, and very good, and my fourth-grader latched onto the books like no series before. I had read *to* him, and I'd read *with* him. It turns out, the combination of words and art was the hook for him. Seeing him with a book in his hand instead of an iPad still throws me for a loop—and I love it. He's read and re-read each of the books in Nathan Hale's series, and recently he's discovered Doug TenNapel's graphic novels. As a parent and a teacher, I want kids to know how much I love to read—everything from Steinbeck to blogs to textbooks to comic books. A love of reading is a love of reading, with or without pictures.

Over the past decade, the number of graphic novels and comic books intended for classroom use has grown exponentially. However, they're not all created equal. A lot of these books are cranked out by textbook publishing houses that pair a simple, poorly-written text with illustrations to create a "graphic novel." Be very selective when you look for graphic novels for your classroom. Just because a book has pictures doesn't mean it will engage students. Crap with pictures is still crap.

Technically, a graphic novel is more than just pictures with text beside it. I use the terms *graphic novel* and *comic book* interchangeably, mostly because a lot of teachers, librarians, and parents still aren't quite sure what a graphic novel is. A graphic novel usually meets the following criteria:

- A graphic novel is an original story told through a sequence of images. It's not just a prose book with an illustration every few pages, even if those illustrations are done in comic book-style artwork.
- A graphic novel is a long-form story with a beginning and end. A single issue of a comic book isn't a graphic novel, though some graphic novels are published in comic book chapters or installments over a period of several months. This shouldn't disqualify them from being considered literature any more than Dickens' works originally published as chapters in newspapers should be.

- Graphic novels are distinguishable from a bound collection of comic strips. I love *Peanuts* and *Calvin and Hobbes*, but they're a serial format without an ending. While they'll sometimes present a long-form story running for a few weeks, ultimately they're no more a graphic novel than an ongoing newspaper column is a book.
- Graphic novels can be fiction or non-fiction, including science fiction, biographies, superheroes, or travelogues. In publishing, a "novel" is usually a fictional story meeting certain parameters. Parameters become a little more loosey-goosey once comic books are part of the equation.
- A graphic novel has the same elements of literature that a good "regular" novel has. Characterization, voice, conflict, plot, climax, conclusion, and the characters should be as complicated as those of a well-written novel. The story is just told differently.
- The real beauty of a graphic novel is found in the way the words and the artwork together tell a story that couldn't be told without the other. Normal prose books rely on the words to paint the pictures and do so beautifully. A graphic novel uses artwork to interpret the visuals, adding layers of meaning and symbolism to what may be more succinct language. We see the setting instead of reading words describing it, but it doesn't make the setting any less important.

The Graphic Advantage,
School Library Journal

But This Book Has Pictures,
AP Central

Many teachers, school librarians, and parents still have issues with comic books and graphic novels, concerned that they're less rigorous than textbooks, or worse, not really books at all. But the reality is that comic books and graphic novels may be more effective teaching tools. Why? If you give a class a textbook, the students will skim the book, looking for answers to fill in the blanks on a worksheet. If you give a class a graphic novel that explores the same content, the students with the graphic novel read, see, and absorb more because graphic novels and comic books tend to be more engaging than a traditional textbook or prose novel. For some students, the visual element provides additional clues about what's happening in the text, while others just find them more appealing than a block of text.

Reluctance to accept graphic novels often comes from teachers who haven't personally read them. Even though most teachers are master readers of textbooks, novels, and other books (for many of us, a love for reading led us to teaching in the first place), reading a comic book or graphic novel is a different kind of literacy. Even finding the sequence of the panels on the page is hard for some of us. While most books are read left-to-right and top-to-bottom, good graphic novels use their art to tell part of the story, not just captions to pictures. You can't separate the art from the script and have a complete story. Since we want students to read and comprehend textbooks, it seems only fair we be able to read and comprehend graphic novels.

General Strategies for Using Graphic Novels and Comics in the Classroom

I've used graphic novels with my students in numerous ways. Some of my favorite strategies include sampling, storyboard creation, text sets, and student collaboration.

Sampling. Each student receives a few panels from a graphic novel they'll be reading in class the following day. You can choose to let the students do a cold read of their panels or give them a brief introduction to the book, so they'll know the general direction of the story. After the students read their section, they predict what happened before and after. With a partner or small group, students share the content of their sections and their predictions. After putting their panels together as a group, if they agree on a sequence of events, students can change their predictions. This activity primes them to read the entire story, and they eagerly look forward to reading their own section.

Storyboard. Each student creates a single page of a graphic novel with a dozen or so panels. Doing this as a class project allows each student to make one page of a final book. The book could tell a single narrative or be informational non-fiction about a particular theme. Publish the finished work on a class website so students can share it with parents and friends.

Text sets. Include graphic novels (or sections of them) and comic books as pieces of text sets, alongside traditional textbook entries, essays, poetry, and other forms of writing. While this won't be possible for every topic, the explosion of young adult graphic novels in recent years has greatly increased the variety of topics available.

Student collaboration. Take advantage of the collaborative nature of graphic novels. If one student is better at writing and another excels at drawing, let them work together to create something better than either could do on his or her own. Creating comics is the perfect place for collaboration.

Writing Comic Books

Just as reading comic books can engage reluctant readers, many teachers have discovered that creating comic books may engage reluctant writers. Personally, I believe every student should be encouraged to write *and* draw, so I often include a drawing component in assignments—sometimes simple, sometimes more elaborate, extended projects. Having that drawing component serves a few purposes—if a student felt like they weren't able to express themselves in writing, this would give them another avenue to convey their understanding. It gives them a chance to graphically represent their thinking. As a teacher, it's sometimes easier to quickly look at an image and see if a kid understood a concept than to decipher their writing. There's a literacy with images that's as critical as a literacy with words. Our visual learners need a chance to exercise those cognitive muscles. Finally, it's fun. And if I, as a teacher, model it and make it more fun, they'll follow.

Many kids enjoy drawing, but they don't connect it with composition. There are some who would write and illustrate a two-page comic book but wouldn't write more than a few sentences on a standard writing assignment. But, by breaking up a story into twenty-five different two-page sections—using the storyboard strategy—your class just wrote a comic book! Sure, the art style changes throughout the book, as does the writing style, but the collaborative story is a coherent whole. Of course, creating illustrations presents a challenge for kids who don't feel like they're artists, but consider the challenge for students who don't feel they're writers. We expect them to write every day in class. Challenge the "non-artists," too. Chances are good these are the very kids who loved drawing in elementary school. Give them the opportunity to rediscover their love of drawing. Provide guidance and templates—and turn them loose!

GRAPHIC NOVELS I'VE USED

NATHAN HALE'S HAZARDOUS TALES

Although language arts classes are where most reading is taught, I've always believed every teacher is a reading teacher. Through the years, I've found some incredible comic books and graphic novels that fit in well with multiple subjects, including science and history. Additionally, there are biographies that span multiple content areas.

One of my favorite graphic novels series for teaching social studies is *Nathan Hale's Hazardous Tales*, which includes books about the American Revolution, Civil War, the Underground Railroad, Westward Expansion, and World War I. They're well-researched, informative, fun—even funny! Kids love reading them. In fact, reluctant readers will not only read them but also read them multiple times.

Hale sets small stories against the backdrop of big events in American history. The first book tells the story of Nathan Hale (the spy) in the context of the American Revolution—not the whole Revolutionary War, but the small part in which Hale was involved. By explaining Hale's reasons for becoming a spy, his goals, his eventual (and pretty quick) capture, and the impact his execution had on the rest of the war and American history, the author gives his readers a good overview and jumping-off point for the American Revolution. He does the same thing with his book about the Battle of the Ironclads during the Civil War.

One of my favorite books in the *Hazardous Tales* series, and the one I'll share some strategies for, is the third book in the series, *The—* wait for it—*Donner Dinner Party*. (Oh no, he didn't!) Oh, yes he did! Hopefully, your hand just flew to your mouth in a nineteenth-century expression of shock. Or perhaps you clenched your fists or even fainted. Such poor taste! (Oops! Unintentional pun—but I'm leaving it in.) Precisely the sort of reaction you *should* have. Because you're adults and teachers. But your students? The title alone will have 93 percent of them (I've done studies. OK, not really.) devouring it. (Okay—that one's intentional.)

If you didn't get those fantastic puns, here's why you should be appalled at this delightfully distasteful title (sorry, I just can't help myself). *The Donner Dinner Party* tells the tale of the unfortunate group of pioneers on their way to California who get stranded in the Sierra Nevadas. One of many tragedies of the American West, it's one of the few that nearly everyone has heard about. But not because of the deaths. Because of the cannibalism. Hale, who undoubtedly wrote that title with glee, is respectful—even reverent—when it comes to the horrors of the story. While he lightens the mood with the way the story is narrated, he allows the reader to feel all of the sadness you want a student to feel when considering the choices these poor souls had to make. This delicate balance of teaching the history, evoking empathy for historic characters, and creating a fun, sometimes laugh-out-loud funny book makes Nathan Hale a master.

I've used *The Donner Dinner Party* with students in a number of ways. The book, like the historic trip itself, is a series of choices. One bad decision didn't put those men, women, and children in the snows of the Donner Pass—a bunch of bad decisions did: leaving too late in the year, conflict among the group, the disastrous choice of listening to Lansford Hastings. Students can chart these decisions using a graphic organizer and a branching model to explore other scenarios. Getting into the "what-ifs" of history is always a dangerous prospect, but Hale

"I determined never to talk down to the reader. I insisted on using college-level vocabulary. If a kid didn't know what a word meant, he'd get it by the use in the sentence by osmosis. If he had to go to a dictionary, that's not the worst thing in the world."

—Stan Lee

includes enough information that students can play out alternate events with more detail than simply concluding they wouldn't have died. Duh.

As the Donner and Reed families and their fellow travelers come together, Hale has a two-page spread introducing us to all of the individuals who made the trip. We see how many are in each family, the number of animals they had, and the kind of vehicles (large wagon, small wagon, etc.) they had to make the journey. Have students choose three families and predict if they'll survive the journey or not. Ask them to evaluate what factors would contribute to success on this trip. At the end of the book, Hale provides a chart showing every individual—survivors highlighted in one color, those who didn't make it in another color. He also tells how those who died lost their lives (disease, violence, cannibalism). Let's face it—that's what your students (and you—don't pretend you're not) are morbidly curious about. Curious enough to read an entire book on the subject. After they finish the book, ask students to evaluate their predictions against the true fate of the families they chose.

After students read *The Donner Dinner Party*, have them write a letter to a friend "back East" who plans on making the same trip the

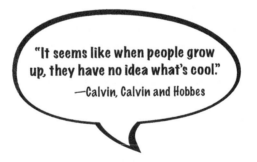

"It seems like when people grow up, they have no idea what's cool."
—Calvin, Calvin and Hobbes

following year. What ten things would they advise their friend to pack? What other advice would a survivor of the Donner Party give to someone making that journey?

The Donner Pass remains one of the only routes through that part of the Sierra Nevada mountain range. Challenge students to design a memorial to the tragedy of the Donner Party and explain their design choices. Along with the design, students can write a brief description of events to display for a plaque at the memorial site.

One point raised in *The Donner Dinner Party* is that resorting to cannibalism in life-or-death circumstances wasn't an unusual survival tactic at the time. Even though twenty-first century readers find the events shocking (and they were salacious news back then, too), it happened regularly enough in maritime disasters to become known as "the custom of the sea." It's terrible, to be sure, but it wasn't unheard of. If your class wants to go down this dark path, they could research other similar events and explain why the Donner Party is the one everyone remembers and talks about, when the other instances seem to have been forgotten.

Oh, and when your class gets to the Donner Pass part in the book, open up a bag of beef jerky, and—I'm kidding. Use bacon.

Wordless Picture Books

OWLY

A unique challenge could be using a wordless comic book. *Owly* by Andy Runton is one of my favorite series for elementary-aged kids (and up!). Criminally cute and completely wordless, the books tell the story of an owl who likes gardening, makes unlikely friends with a worm, and faces challenges with aplomb. The stories have a similar spirit to *Winnie the Pooh*. Best of all, they communicate complex stories with imagery. While there are occasional word or thought bubbles, they contain only symbols, like light bulbs and exclamation points.

One suggestion for using wordless comic books with your students is to assign each student four pages of the book and have them draw what they imagine happened before their four pages and what they believe will happen after them. When they've completed their drawings, share the rest of the story and see if their predictions were correct. If they weren't correct, ask them to gauge their story against the author's version and determine which they liked best.

Another idea is to have students work with just a few pages again, but this time fill in the speech bubbles in the book. How can those add depth and characterization to the original story? Alternatively, have them create speech bubbles telling a completely different story than what the author was intending but which could still be supported by the pictures.

Andy Runton's Free Comic Book Day Stories

As I've mentioned, I'm a fan of students drawing in class, and the simple lines of the *Owly* books provide a good template for students to use to create their own wordless comics. In fact, this template seems especially appropriate for demonstrating a concept with several steps, for example, the process of photosynthesis, the events at the climax of a novel, the stages toward a revolution, or the need for and discovery of a new invention.

THE ARRIVAL

Another favorite wordless graphic novel is Shaun Tan's *The Arrival*. Where *Owly* is an all-ages book geared more towards primary grades, *The Arrival*, while squeaky-clean, is clearly for older students. An Australian artist, Tan has created a universal immigration story. The protagonist leaves his home and family. Why? We don't know. But there are spined tentacles curling around the corners of his neighborhood. Are these tentacles a literal monster, or do they represent unemployment, political turmoil, or famine? We don't know. We don't know where he's moving from, but he travels to a distant country, someplace—different—not Australia or the United States. The protagonist has to learn to navigate an entirely new world and recreate his life, including finding a new home, finding a job, learning to eat, making new friends, and eventually reuniting with his family who joins him.

Arrival is 128 pages long, each hauntingly beautiful. Tan creates allegories of Ellis Island, but completely unique, and an alphabet in the New World resembling the Roman, Hebrew, Arabic, or Cyrillic alphabets, yet it is none of those. The foods, animals, transportation, clothing—all are familiar, yet different enough to confuse the reader. Which makes it a perfect example of an immigration experience. As a social studies teacher, I loved it. As a human being, I loved it.

While it's not always realistic for teachers to purchase classroom sets of books, *The Arrival* is so gorgeous, you'll want a class set because students will pore over every detail of every page. When I first discovered the book, I couldn't afford to buy a classroom set, so I used strategies I could do with one copy. For example, I gave each student passages of the book representing a certain facet of the immigration experience, and they wrote dialogue for the protagonist as he goes through the process of assimilating that aspect of his new life. Some is actual dialogue between characters, but much of it is an inner monologue represented by "thought balloons" in traditional comic books.

I destroyed a copy of *The Arrival*, cutting it up and mounting it onto poster boards. I shuffled the immigration experience, and students worked in groups to reassemble the storyline and justify their ordering of events. For example, why would the protagonist need to get a job before he found a place to live?

After acquiring a classroom set of the books, I wanted to test my assertion that Tan had written a universal immigration story. I gave each student three pieces of text excerpted from first-person accounts of immigrants traveling to and from countries on all six continents. At least one of the three was written by someone coming to the United States, and no two students had the same three texts. Their task was to "read" *The Arrival* and insert pieces of text where those non-fiction words made the most sense in the fictional book.

I continually challenge my students to find the answer to this question: "Why are you here?" ("Here" being Utah.) You have to have a reason to end up in the Beehive State. I love Utah, but it's weird. And kids realize that. So the personal immigration stories of my students and their families became part of our history studies. For one term project, my students interviewed their parents, grandparents, or other relatives to learn their family's story. One of their options was to include an illustration of part of their ancestors' experience in the style of *The Arrival*—the weirder, the better, as long as the story was clear.

OTHER GRAPHIC NOVEL AND COMIC BOOK RECOMMENDATIONS

What started as a "top ten" list for elementary students and a separate top ten list for secondary students turned into a list of nearly forty books. I can't narrow it down more than this. I've tried. Keep in mind that many of the elementary books listed are also read and loved by older students. However, the ones on the secondary list have themes, content, or vocabulary that may be inappropriate for elementary students, depending on your students, parents, community, and you. As with any material you're using in class, read it first. They're your kids. You'll know what works with them.

ELEMENTARY RECOMMENDATIONS

Amulet (series) by Kazu Kibuishi

Emily and her brother Navin leave our world for a more magical one after their father dies, encountering elves, monsters, sentient foxes, cats, and, of course, an amulet of incredible power.

Bone (series) by Jeff Smith

The ultimate hero's quest—in the form of a cute, shapeless, little guy with staunch allies and despicable enemies.

Cardboard by Doug TenNapel

A single dad gives his son some magical cardboard; everything they build with it comes to life.

Cleopatra in Space (series) by Mike Maihack

Cleopatra of ancient Egypt gets transported into the distant future, where she learns to be a real leader. She has to save the galaxy—and get good grades at the same time.

Fable Comics/Fairy Tale Comics/Nursery Rhyme Comics by Chris Duffy

Anthologies of classic tales retold by dozens of different comic book writers and artists. It's a good choice for even the youngest readers.

Mouse Guard (series) by David Petersen

A medieval civilization of mice deals with the challenges of building and defending their kingdoms and castles. Beautifully illustrated.

Nathan Hale's Hazardous Tales (series) by Nathan Hale

My favorite series about American history, narrated by the hanged spy Nathan Hale. Informative, detailed, and funny. Kids love it—and so do their history teachers.

OWLY (SERIES) BY ANDY RUNTON

Wordless books about an adorable owl who makes unlikely friends.

PRIMATES: THE FEARLESS SCIENCE OF JANE GOODALL, DIAN FOSSEY, AND BIRUTE GALDIKAS BY JIM OTTAVIANI

The biographies and discoveries of three scientists who changed our understanding of chimpanzees, gorillas, and orangutans.

RAPUNZEL'S REVENGE BY SHANNON HALE

The classic fairy tale retold in a Wild West setting, with one of the strongest heroines in comics.

SHAZAM AND THE MONSTER SOCIETY OF EVIL BY JEFF SMITH

The story of a boy who cries *"Shazam!"* and becomes Captain Marvel, with superpowers as great as Superman.

SUPERMAN FOR ALL SEASONS BY JEPH LOEB

Superman's origin story from Smallville to Metropolis, told from the perspective of his allies and enemies.

THE WONDERFUL WIZARD OF OZ (SERIES) BY ERIC SHANOWER AND SKOTTIE YOUNG

Excellent retellings of the classic L. Frank Baum stories by an Oz expert, with fresh artwork creating an incredible new world we want to explore.

SECONDARY RECOMMENDATIONS

ACTION PHILOSOPHERS BY FRED VAN LENTE

Anthology of the lives and ideas of some of the world's greatest thinkers—wrestlers, superheroes (anything but boring old guys)—in comic book format.

American Born Chinese by Gene Luen Yang

A Chinese-American boy comes to terms with his identity in this irreverent and often very funny book.

Anne Frank: The Anne Frank House Authorized Graphic Biography by Sid Jacobson

This biography starts with the famous diary but moves beyond those pages to give us more insight into the lives of her family, friends, and community.

Anya's Ghost by Vera Brosgol

A ghost story set in a modern high school. The female hero and villain both have a strong voice.

The Arrival by Shaun Tan

A wordless "universal immigration story" told with abstract artwork, giving the reader a sense of disorientation likely felt by those moving to a new country.

Batgirl: Year One by Scott Beatty

The first year of Barbara Gordon's time as a superhero, told from her perspective. Exciting, and funnier than you'd expect.

Batman: The Long Halloween by Jeph Loeb

This is one of the best Batman books for someone new to reading comic books. The yearlong mystery of a serial killer in Gotham City introduces every classic Batman villain with incredible artwork and a compelling story.

Blankets by Craig Thompson

A coming-of-age story, *Blankets* is about a young man wrestling with issues of family, religion, friendship, and identity.

CAPTAIN MARVEL (SERIES) BY KELLY SUE DECONNICK

The story of Carol Danvers, one of the Avengers and one of the strongest heroes in the Marvel universe, told with a fresh voice which doesn't pull any punches.

CHARLES DARWIN'S ON THE ORIGIN OF SPECIES: A GRAPHIC ADAPTATION BY MICHAEL KELLER

A beautifully illustrated version of the groundbreaking work, using many of Darwin's own words, and giving us insight into his biography.

THE GETTYSBURG ADDRESS: A GRAPHIC ADAPTATION BY JONATHAN HENNESSEY

Hennessey uses the words of the Gettysburg Address as a jumping-off point to teach all of American history, from the American Revolution through the twenty-first century.

GOTHAM ACADEMY (SERIES) BY BECKY CLOONAN

Set in a boarding school in Gotham City, this mystery takes place in Batman's shadow but doesn't have much Batman in it. Featuring unforgettable new characters and a fun story, it will hook kids and adults.

LEWIS AND CLARK BY NICK BERTOZZI

The best of many different retellings of the Corps of Discovery, it examines not only the journey but also the personal lives and trials of these American heroes.

MARCH BY JOHN LEWIS

This graphic novel revisits the events of the Civil Rights Movement. It's written by one of its major players.

MAUS: A SURVIVOR'S TALE BY ART SPIEGELMAN

This is the Holocaust book that convinced millions of teachers to take comic books seriously. Groundbreaking when it was written, it is still one of the best history graphic novels available.

MS. MARVEL (SERIES) BY G. WILLOW WILSON

This tells the story of Kamala Khan, a Muslim high school girl living in Jersey City who gets superpowers but still has to navigate issues of school and family. She sets up secret headquarters in the corner convenience store.

THE SCULPTOR BY SCOTT MCCLOUD

An incredible story about an artist who sells his soul for the ability to sculpt anything from any material; it explores ideas about love, art, life, and death.

SUPERMAN: BIRTHRIGHT BY MARK WAID

A retelling of Superman's origin story, this story makes Clark Kent more human than he's ever been and Superman more super because of it.

TRINITY: A GRAPHIC HISTORY OF THE FIRST ATOMIC BOMB BY JONATHAN FETTER-VORM

This examination of the Manhattan Project includes a biography of Oppenheimer and a look at the science of the atom bomb like you've never seen it before.

THE UNDERWATER WELDER BY JEFF LEMIRE

This is a story about fathers and sons and how problematic relationships can be passed down from generation to generation—or not.

V FOR VENDETTA BY ALAN MOORE

London is in the grips of an Orwellian nightmare, until a vigilante and his young protégé decide to take matters into their own hands.

WATCHMEN BY ALAN MOORE

Superheroes are being killed off one by one in a dark future. Can some former heroes solve the mystery in time to save their own lives—and the entire planet?

My Graphic Novel and Comic Book Recommendations

No Flying, No Tights: A Graphic Novel Review Blog

USING POP CULTURE TO TEACH

While this book focuses on the toys, games, and comic books of pop culture, some teachers are taking their love of two of my biggest pop culture touchstones—*Star Wars* and *Star Trek* (Yes, you can be a fan of both!)—into the classroom in other ways that I love! *Star Wars* in the Classroom is a group of hundreds of teachers who call themselves Rogues, after a squadron of Rebel Alliance pilots. One of the best-organized and far-reaching of this type of group, the Rogues share lesson plans about social studies, language arts, robotics, mythology, science, music, health—they have a lesson plan for almost every content area. And even though some students may not like *Star Wars*, most of them have seen the movies or are at least familiar with them. So, when I used an example of the Ewoks fighting the Empire in *Return of the Jedi* to teach my Vietnam unit, my students had some immediate frame of reference. But some of these teachers take things even further and are doing amazing things in their classrooms. For example, some teachers use *Star Wars* to teach literary elements of Shakespeare using Ian Doescher's *William Shakespeare's Star Wars* series of books. Others use *Star Wars'* many aliens and monsters to teach biodiversity and taxonomy. Anyone teaching the classical Hero's Journey could (and should) use the life of Luke Skywalker as a prime example. These teachers are using the *Star Wars* movies as a scaffold to get to their actual "content," and it works beautifully.

The first time I saw an episode of *Star Trek*, I was in a science class. My teacher used the classic episode, "Devil in the Dark" (with the lava monster that was killing people under the planet's surface but turned out to be a mama protecting her eggs) to teach what life on different planets could be like. What a great way to illustrate how, instead of taking the shapes we're familiar with, alien life forms could be completely different.

Using examples from pop culture can make the abstract more real to students. Maybe this seems backwards, but with all the time we spend plugged in, it may just be that Yoda has more relevance than Gandhi and may be a better teaching model for some topics. Come to think of it, Yoda and Gandhi dress similarly, both use walking sticks, have a similar message, and have never been in the same place at the same time—wait a minute!

Star Wars
in the Classroom

HISTORY OF COMIC STRIPS

Comic strips began in the late nineteenth century, with the expansion of newspapers in Europe and the United States. Some of the earliest have also had the longest lifespans, including the *Katzenjammer Kids*, *Little Orphan Annie*, *Popeye*, *Gasoline Alley*, and *Blondie*. While most comic strips are comic (humor right there in the name!), there are also adventure strips that have included great characters, such as Tarzan, Flash Gordon, and the Lone Ranger. Some of them tied in with radio or television shows, some of them are just there to sell products, and some have turned into generational soap operas with sprawling casts. There are as many kinds of comic strips as there are artists. As newspaper circulation has plummeted in recent years, many artists have moved to "webcomics," which have the same essential principles as classic comic strips but are also free of the restrictions that newspapers put on them. Their space is virtually unlimited, they can publish on their own schedule, and they won't have an editor breathing down their neck. Comic strips will survive, even if newspapers (as such) don't.

14

COMIC STRIPS

Growing up, my parents were newspaper readers. That made me want to be a newspaper reader. The part with the most pictures (aside from the obituaries, which were also interesting) was the comics page. I've loved *Peanuts* for as long as I can remember. Even if I didn't always understand Charlie Brown's existential angst, he had a dog, I had a dog, and I loved thinking about my dog flying an airplane. I loved *Family Circus* so much that my mom would sometimes clip the cartoon from the morning paper and put it in my lunch, so I'd have a smile in the middle of the school day. Later on, *Calvin and Hobbes* became my favorite, as I saw that there were other kids out there, like me, who would rather spend their time daydreaming about adventures with their Rubber Duckie (I mean, stuffed tiger) than focusing on their math problems. Other strips, like *Bloom County* and *Doonesbury* had me asking adults what words meant, or who politicians were, and learning quickly that not all adults had the same political views as a cartoonist. Comic strips were a huge part of my childhood. Going back and reading them in collected book editions today makes me smile because they're still funny—and because of the nostalgia of little Quinn growing up with some of his best friends.

COMICS IN THE CLASSROOM

A close relative of graphic novels and comic books, comic strips have the benefit of being succinct, telling a story in a few panels. While they seem to be waning as the newspaper medium is losing ground, some comic strips have become pop culture icons and will be around forever. *Peanuts, Calvin and Hobbes,* and *The Far Side* are a few of my personal favorites. Regardless of the comic strip, the format is similar: the character has a conflict, and the conflict has a resolution, which usually involves a play on words or a sight gag. Most cartoonists use three or four panels; *The Far Side* creator, Gary Larson, used only one. Here are just a few examples of how you can use comic strips in the classroom:

Start with a laugh. Comic strips can be a "starter" for your class. Find one connected to your content. If you have to stretch to make the

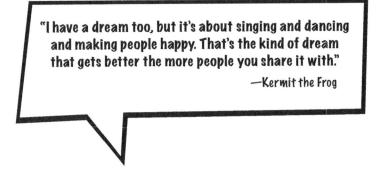

connection, it's likely funnier than if the strip is specifically related to the topic. That said, *The Far Side* strips are frequently used as a source of science jokes. If you're a science teacher and aren't using them, you're committing a crime against comedy.

Say it for them. Another activity is to blank out the word balloons in a comic strip and ask students to predict what the characters are

saying. Let them evaluate their version against what the artist originally wrote to determine which they like better.

Qu'a-t-il dit? (What did he say?) In a foreign language class, students can translate comic strips from English into the target language.
Humor is one of the most difficult things to translate. (When I lived
in Germany, I felt like I finally understood the language when I was
funny–or as funny as I was in English. Which is pretty funny—just ask
me.) Using comic strips in a foreign language class has the dual benefit
of being a short piece of text *and* having the comedic payoff. If students' translations aren't quite right or aren't really funny in the target
language, they still gain experience, and the activity is different from
their typical language exercises. *Calvin and Hobbes* was very popular
when I lived in Germany. Reading those strips in my target language
helped my vocabulary *and* my "German sense of humor."

Write the story. Most comic strips have the climax, or punch line,
in the last panel. Since most daily strips carry a storyline from Monday
to Saturday, the story continues after each punch line. With this in
mind, give your students a comic strip and ask them to predict what
will happen next by adding three more panels to the strip.

As with many other comic books and comic strips intended for
classroom use, some great online tools are available to help students
create their own. If students aren't comfortable creating in pen and ink,
encourage them to use pixels—it gets you to the same goal.

STORYTELLING

Storytelling is one of the best tools in your teacher toy box. I think most teachers—once they get into their groove with their students—are master storytellers. My personal favorite approach to storytelling usually involves stretching a story until it breaks—or at least until a student calls me on it. My all-time best story stretcher featured the Majestic Bagelope. When the brave pioneers headed west across the Oregon Trail, Santa Fe Trail, and Mormon Trail, they'd see bison, prairie dogs, and bagelopes—little critters about six inches tall, with flattened, round bodies and an improbable hole right through the middle of their torsos. The pioneers would scoop them up, snap off their twig-like legs and antlers, and eat them. Sometimes with a little bit of cream cheese! Of course I was pulling their legs, but watching middle school kids' eyes get bigger and bigger as I told the tale convinced me I'd hooked them into talking about the real topic of the day. I've also drawn an artist's depiction and recently built a "stuffed" bagelope—whatever it takes to sell the story.

And when the kids leave my class, they exit through the gateway into Narnia, but that's a story for another time.

14

Conclusion

> "When I was young, my ambition was to be one of the people who made a difference in the world. My hope is to leave the world a little better for having been there."
>
> —Jim Henson

I just spent a bunch of pages talking about how much I love toys, games, and comics. And I do—a lot! They're fun for me—even as an adult outside of the classroom. Plus, they engage my students inside the classroom. If you combine some of these strategies with your own kids and curriculum, you'll discover a bundle of activities to engage your students as well. Not only will they love them, *you'll* have fun, too!

But hopefully the message of this book goes beyond the toys, games, and comics. The real message is about using your own personal passions to teach. I get stoked about toys. You may get jazzed by music, sports, travel, or poetry. Whatever your passion, you can find ways to bring it into your classroom and make your lessons different from the teacher's next door. Your class will be something kids remember.

You'll do incredible things! As a student, I made it through the educational system unscathed, but I was rarely engaged—rarely curious. Using your own interests, hobbies, and passions, you'll reach students in ways you never thought possible. And on the way, you'll teach them the math and science and everything else you're supposed to teach them. But the best thing? They'll actually learn the content, connect with it—and connect with you.

Teaching makes me happy; it energizes me. In fact, there are few things in life I enjoy more. Hopefully, you feel the same. As you bring more of *you* into your classroom, you'll discover your energy, effectiveness, and, most of all, your happiness increases. Teaching should be your life—not just your job. As you connect your life to your class, you'll grow and love each school day, even the challenging ones. Even more important, your kids will come to love school as much as you do.

BE THAT ROCK STAR

It's okay to be awesome. The way I teach isn't for every teacher or for every student. But I have a blast doing it. And I honestly think I'm an awesome teacher. I'm not saying that out of arrogance or superiority—I know I still have a lot to learn and there are some things I don't do well. But I want my students to know I think of myself as a good teacher, and I want them to look forward to my class. It's also important to me that I do my job well—as a professional and as a husband and father. I want my family to think of me as a great teacher—as someone who is excited about my classes and students and who loves his career. Teaching is the best job there is. Commit to be the best teacher you can be. Don't apologize for being awesome. Be that rock star.

Acknowledgments

First and foremost, I thank my wife, Melissa. She's more patient than she needs to be and understands me and my geeky obsessions—even when she doesn't want to. I owe her my life; without her, I never would've become a teacher.

My sons, Miles and Carter, have become my partners in crime over the years—whether we're hiking, LEGOing, or binge-watching a geeky show. I'll always cherish the bonds we share. (Oh, and boys—every LEGO gift you've ever received reverts back to the purchaser [me!] if you haven't played with it for six months. There—now it's in writing. Sorry, boys.)

My parents, my sister, my brother, and my in-laws have been enablers for as long as I can remember—giving me toys for Christmas and birthdays well into my teens. And twenties. And thirties. And forties. You get the idea. They've supported me in every creative and obsessive endeavor I've engaged in, and I'll always be grateful to them.

The teachers, students, and families at Bennion Junior High will always be precious to me. They supported and loved me from my first year as a teacher, shaping me into the teacher I've become. I've been fortunate to land among supportive teachers at the school, district, and state level. And my fellow teachers, principals, and other administrators have been willing to let me be the one with the noisy class—the one trying new ideas. Their willingness opened doors for me I wouldn't have opened on my own and helped me find the path to being a teacher-leader. Mary Rhodes, Dawn Hauser, Pam Su'a, and Robert Austin have been invaluable as leaders and friends, and I'll always appreciate what they've done for me.

A few years ago, I discovered the Personal Learning Network (PLN) model, connecting teachers across the country and around the world through Twitter. Members of the Social Studies Chat (#sschat) and the Teach Like a PIRATE Chat (#tlap) groups have been an endless source of inspiration and support. The friends and resources I found through this PLN have changed my professional life.

Thanks to Robert Atkins, whose templates for superheroes have been used by teachers and students across the country. He does amazing work, and I appreciate his support of children, education, and geeks everywhere.

Finally, I need to thank Dave Burgess, who put into words the "teaching like a pirate" I felt I was already doing before I read his book or met him in person. He gave me more ideas, more resources, and more authority to experiment with tools that I thought were best for my students. Dave is a force of nature. I'll be forever grateful he happened to see my presentation about using toys, comics, and games in the classroom, liked it, and asked me if I wanted to write a book.

Every word I just wrote about Dave applies to Shelley Burgess as well. She's been an incredible support through this process. She and Erin Casey's editorial team helped me write a book with more clarity than my first drafts but which still had my voice. Plus, they kept most of my jokes—even the ones they shouldn't have. Squeaked it by them. I can think of no other team doing more to lead teachers than Dave Burgess' crew, and I'm honored to be part of it.

More from

DAVE BURGESS Consulting, Inc.

Teach Like a PIRATE

Increase Student Engagement, Boost Your Creativity, and Transform Your Life as an Educator

By Dave Burgess (@BurgessDave)

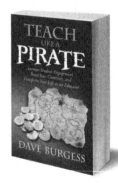

Teach Like a PIRATE is the *New York Times'* best-selling book that has sparked a worldwide educational revolution. It is part inspirational manifesto that ignites passion for the profession and part practical road map, filled with dynamic strategies to dramatically increase student engagement. Translated into multiple languages, its message resonates with educators who want to design outrageously creative lessons and transform school into a life-changing experience for students.

P is for PIRATE

Inspirational ABC's for Educators
By Dave and Shelley Burgess
(@Burgess_Shelley)

Teaching is an adventure that stretches the imagination and calls for creativity every day! In *P is for Pirate*, husband and wife team, Dave and Shelley Burgess, encourage and inspire educators to make their classrooms fun and exciting places to learn. Tapping into years of personal experience and drawing on the insights of more than seventy educators, the authors offer a wealth of ideas for making learning and teaching more fulfilling than ever before.

Ditch That Textbook

*Free Your Teaching and
Revolutionize Your Classroom*
By Matt Miller (@jmattmiller)

Textbooks are symbols of centuries of old education. They're often outdated as soon as they hit students' desks. Acting "by the textbook" implies compliance and a lack of creativity. It's time to ditch those textbooks—and those textbook assumptions about learning! In *Ditch That Textbook*, teacher and blogger Matt Miller encourages educators to throw out meaningless, pedestrian teaching and learning practices. He empowers them to evolve and improve on old, standard, teaching methods. *Ditch That Textbook* is a support system, toolbox, and manifesto to help educators free their teaching and revolutionize their classrooms.

Learn Like a PIRATE
Empower Your Students to
Collaborate, Lead, and Succeed
By Paul Solarz (@PaulSolarz)

Today's job market demands that students be prepared to take responsibility for their lives and careers. We do them a disservice if we teach them how to earn passing grades without equipping them to take charge of their education. In *Learn Like a Pirate*, Paul Solarz explains how to design classroom experiences that encourage students to take risks and explore their passions in a stimulating, motivating, and supportive environment where improvement, rather than grades, is the focus. Discover how student-led classrooms help students thrive and develop into self-directed, confident citizens who are capable of making smart, responsible decisions, all on their own.

Pure Genius
Building a Culture of Innovation and
Taking 20% Time to the Next Level
By Don Wettrick (@DonWettrick)

For far too long, schools have been bastions of boredom, killers of creativity, and way too comfortable with compliance and conformity. In *Pure Genius*, Don Wettrick explains how collaboration—with experts, students, and other educators—can help you create interesting, and even life-changing, opportunities for learning. Wettrick's book inspires and equips educators with a systematic blueprint for teaching innovation in any school.

50 Things You Can Do with Google Classroom
By Alice Keeler and Libbi Miller
(@AliceKeeler, @MillerLibbi)

It can be challenging to add new technology to the classroom, but it's a must if students are going to be well-equipped for the future. Alice Keeler and Libbi Miller shorten the learning curve by providing a thorough overview of the Google Classroom App. Part of Google Apps for Education (GAfE), Google Classroom was specifically designed to help teachers save time by streamlining the process of going digital. Complete with screenshots, *50 Things You Can Do with Google Classroom* provides ideas and step-by-step instructions to help teachers implement this powerful tool.

The Zen Teacher
Creating FOCUS, SIMPLICITY, and TRANQUILITY in the Classroom
By Dan Tricarico (@TheZenTeacher)

Teachers have incredible power to influence, even improve, the future. In *The Zen Teacher*, educator, blogger, and speaker Dan Tricarico provides practical, easy-to-use techniques to help teachers be their best—unrushed and fully focused—so they can maximize their performance and improve their quality of life. In this introductory guide, Dan Tricarico explains what it means to develop a Zen practice—something that has nothing to do with religion and everything to do with your ability to thrive in the classroom.

Master the Media
How Teaching Media Literacy Can Save
Our Plugged-in World
By Julie Smith (@julnilsmith)

Written to help teachers and parents
educate the next generation, *Master the
Media* explains the history, purpose, and
messages behind the media. The point isn't
to get kids to unplug; it's to help them make informed choices, understand the difference between truth and lies, and discern perception
from reality. Critical thinking leads to smarter decisions—and it's why
media literacy can save the world.

Your School Rocks... So Tell People!
*Passionately Pitch and Promote the
Positives Happening on Your Campus*
By Ryan McLane and Eric Lowe
(@McLane_Ryan, @EricLowe21)

Great things are happening in your
school every day. The problem is: no one
beyond your school walls knows about them. School principals Ryan
McLane and Eric Lowe want to help you get the word out! In *Your
School Rocks...So Tell People!*, McLane and Lowe offer more than seventy immediately actionable tips along with easy-to-follow instructions and links to video tutorials. This practical guide will equip you
to create an effective and manageable communication strategy using
social media tools. Learn how to keep your students' families and
community connected, informed, and excited about what's going on
in your school.

eXPLORE LIKE A PIRATE

Gamification and Game-Inspired Course Design to Engage, Enrich, and Elevate Your Learners
By Michael Matera (@MrMatera)

Are you ready to transform your classroom into an experiential world that flourishes on collaboration and creativity? Then set sail with classroom game designer and educator, Michael Matera, as he reveals the possibilities and power of game-based learning. In eXPlore like a Pirate, Matera serves as your experienced guide to help you apply the most motivational techniques of gameplay to your classroom. You'll learn gamification strategies that will work with and enhance (rather than replace) your current curriculum and discover how these engaging methods can be applied to any grade level or subject.

The Innovator's Mindset

Empower Learning, Unleash Talent, and Lead a Culture of Creativity
By George Couros (@gcouros)

The traditional system of education requires students to hold their questions and compliantly stick to the scheduled curriculum. But our job as educators is to provide new and better opportunities for our students. It's time to recognize that compliance doesn't foster innovation, encourage critical thinking, or inspire creativity—and those are the skills our students need to succeed. In *The Innovator's Mindset*, George Couros encourages teachers and administrators to empower their learners to wonder, to explore—and to become forward-thinking leaders.

About the Author

Quinn Rollins has been a social studies teacher in Granite School District in Salt Lake City since 2004, where he currently serves as the social studies curriculum specialist. Whether teaching children or adults, he believes in engaging students with humor, pop culture, and new perspectives. As a result, he's been honored to work with the educational programs for the University of Utah, Utah State University, Brigham Young University-Idaho, and Westminster College of Salt Lake City. Quinn has also served as master teacher and mentor for a Teaching American History Grant and for a National Endowment for the Humanities Landmarks of American History Workshop in Chicago, Illinois.

In 2011, he received the Utah Council for the Social Studies Secondary Teacher of the Year award. In 2015, he was presented with "Utah's Best of the West" award at the National Council for the Social Studies conference and the Best Historical Scene and Best Custom Minifigures awards at BrickSlopes 2015, Utah's LEGO Convention.

Quinn loves presenting at local, state, and national conferences. His most popular presentations include student engagement, teaching with pop culture, the literacy of comic books and graphic novels, and using toys to teach.

Quinn's hobbies include designing and playing with toys, doodling in staff meetings, reading comic books, and let's say "running" to sound like a well-rounded person. He believes cheese is "an enemy to mankind" but won't say no to pizza.

He earned his bachelor's degrees in History Teaching and German Teaching and his master's degree in Instructional Design and Educational Technology from the University of Utah.

You can connect with Quinn at QuinnRollins.com and on Twitter @jedikermit.

About the Duck

Rubber Duckie has been traveling with Quinn Rollins since summer of 1990. He's often referred to as a sidekick but considers himself an equal partner in their adventures. He's been in the Atlantic Ocean, Pacific Ocean, Gulf of Mexico, the Colorado, Mississippi, Rhine, and Thames Rivers, but, oddly enough, is afraid of water. Over the last several decades, Rubber Duckie has been kidnapped, searched by multiple TSA agents, and was the target of an NYPD operation in 2002. He made his national television debut on *Who Wants To Be a Millionaire* and is also available for squeaking engagements.

Keep up with Rubber Duckie's adventures by liking his Facebook Page Facebook.com/DuckieTravels.

Made in the USA
Coppell, TX
02 May 2022

77311377R00095